WAGE POLITICS IN BRITAIN
1945–1967

WAGE POLITICS IN BRITAIN
1945–1967
Government vs. the TUC

G E R A L D   A .   D O R F M A N

THE IOWA STATE UNIVERSITY PRESS / AMES, IOWA

1973

GERALD A. DORFMAN is Assistant Professor, Department of Political Science, Iowa State University. He holds the bachelor of science degree from the University of Wisconsin and the master's and doctor of philosophy degrees from Columbia University. His general research interests include British and western European politics and government, and he is both co-founder and publishing director of *Politics and Society,* a scholarly journal in the field of political science.

© 1973 Iowa State University Press
Ames, Iowa 50010. All rights reserved

Composed and printed by
The Iowa State University Press

First edition, 1973

Library of Congress Cataloging in Publication Data

Dorfman, Gerald Allen, 1939–
   Wage politics in Britain, 1945–1967.

   Bibliography: p.
   1. Trades Union Congress. 2. Wage-price policy—Great Britain. 3. Great Britain—Economic policy—1945.
   I. Title.
HD8383.T74D67   331.2′942   72–1833
ISBN 0–8138–0300–4

CONTENTS

ACKNOWLEDGMENTS

I DID an important part of the research for this book in Britain and I acknowledge a debt of gratitude to the many trade union leaders and party officials who generously shared their knowledge and experiences with me. George Woodcock, the former General Secretary of the Trades Union Congress, and Sir Sidney Greene, the General Secretary of the National Union of Railwaymen were particularly helpful. Also I wish to thank the TUC for providing me with working space and free access to its extensive library.

The advice, suggestions, and encouragement of Professor Ira Katznelson of Columbia University and Professor Jorgen Rasmussen of Vanderbilt University have been invaluable. I wish also to acknowledge gratefully the suggestions and comments of professors Karl Fox, Harold Davey, and Donald Boles of Iowa State University.

And, finally, I owe an enormous debt to my wife Penny for her confidence and tireless help.

N O T E

T HE Trades Union Congress (TUC) is the center of the British trade union movement. It represents about 170 unions (of more than 8½ million members) in dealing with government, employers' organizations, and numerous other groups and international unions. At the apex of the TUC's formal structure lies the annual, week-long Congress of member unions that debates resolutions, approves reports, and elects the year-round TUC leadership of the General Council and the TUC General Secretary (elected once, to serve until retirement). Continuous policy is thus made by the General Council (composed of nearly forty constituent union leaders and the TUC General Secretary), together with the advice and assistance of the full-time TUC staff of about one hundred, under the day-to-day direction of the TUC General Secretary.

Although the TUC speaks for its member unions on a broad range of national issues, each union retains full authority to represent its members in their relations with employers. Terms of employment, including wage rates and conditions of work are the subject of negotiations between employers and the separate unions; they are not the responsibility or direct concern of the TUC. A General Secretary or President leads each union, usually elected to serve until retirement by the unions' annual membership meeting. Each General Secretary or President sets union policy (often with the advice of a committee of part-time officials) which is then carried out by a network of full-time local union officials.

At the bottom of the hierarchy, but serving in an exceptionally important way, are the shop stewards who are the unpaid union representatives in the place of work. Formally responsible to the full-time local union officials, shop stewards often supervise agreements worked out by the senior union leadership, negotiate piece-rates and working hours, supervise safety regulations, and collect contributions and handle recruitment as well.

WAGE POLITICS IN BRITAIN
1945–1967

Introduction: A Brief Review

BRITAIN'S troubled economy has been the most pressing domestic issue of its politics during the past half-century. Recession during the twenties was followed by depression during the thirties; then the Second World War stripped away the last vestiges of Britain's nineteenth-century wealth and economic preeminence. Such painful adversities led eventually to the forging of a general consensus about a new economic and social "contract" during the latter part of the war.[1] By this contract, the government committed itself to manage the economy in order to provide full employment; maintain a high and constantly rising standard of living; and keep inflation at a minimum; all the while protecting the value of the pound sterling.[2] Yet, despite these commitments, the British government, more than a quarter-century later, still contends with a lagging and crisis-ridden economy.

Even the briefest examination of British economic history since 1945 demonstrates that more vigorous government intervention in the economy has not achieved the goals posed in the new economic "contract"—with the important exception of full employment. In contrast to the United States, Britain, as a small island nation, still is unable consistently either to produce at home or to sell abroad enough to finance a satisfactory standard of living. The seemingly endless series of balance of payments deficits and economic crises since

---

1. The most influential work in framing the new economic purposes was Beveridge, *Full Employment in a Free Society;* the key public document defining and confirming the commitment to permanent full employment was Ministry of Reconstruction, *Employment Policy,* Cmd. 6527.

2. This list is adapted from Christoph, "The Birth of Neddy," *Cases in Comparative Politics,* Christoph, ed., p. 47.

3

1945, punctuated only by brief periods of surplus, document
this persistent dilemma.

The failure of government to solve or significantly
mitigate the problems contributing to Britain's economic
stagnation has been due in large measure to the continued
high rate of price and wage inflation.[3] Britain so depends on
the condition of its international trading position that inflation, as it increases consumer demand at home and
heightens the costs of goods produced for export, exerts a
decisively negative influence on the country's economic
health. Many observers place the largest share of the blame
for the damaging high rate of wage inflation (and often for
the whole range of Britain's economic problems) squarely on
the trade union movement.[4] These observers charge that the
Trades Union Congress (TUC), the spokesman group for
British unions akin to the AFL-CIO in the United States, is
organizationally weak and ineffective and that the trade
union movement is selfishly insensitive to the larger needs of
the country as compared to its own.

The central concern of this book is to examine the behavior of the TUC in relation to government's efforts between 1945 and 1967 to deal with Britain's economic problems through more direct intervention in the economy.
Full employment, in the context of the managed economy, has been the specific linchpin of the trade union
movement's postwar bargaining relationship with government. The goals of a higher rate of economic growth, of a
strong currency, and a higher standard of living all depend
to a significant extent on trade unionism exercising restraint
in using the leverage for higher wages that full employment
has offered. When the TUC has refused to exercise restraint,
or has been unable to convince its constituent unions or their
members to exercise restraint, government has had to resort

---

3. For an excellent discussion of the relationship of high inflation to Britain's continuing economic problems, see Caves and Associates, *Britain's Economic Prospects*, chaps. I, II, III.
4. For example, see Shanks, *The Stagnant Society;* Shonfield, *Modern Capitalism.*

instead to deflationary measures that more indirectly restrained inflation at the expense of one or several of the goals of its economic policy.

Professor Samuel Beer comments that the wider scope of public policy during the war and under the terms of the new economic contract dictated that government impart much greater power to those groups in the society whose advice it needs to carry out its new responsibilities.[5] Government simply cannot manage the economy "without the advice and cooperation of the great organized producer groups of business, labor, and agriculture."[6] The TUC, as the center of the trade union movement, has thus been endowed by government with effective power to "bargain" the terms of economic policy as part of a new system of producer group politics. However, like the AFL-CIO, the TUC does not negotiate industrial contracts with employers. That function still belongs solely to its member unions, and therein lies a serious problem that complicates the conduct of producer group politics. For although government needs the TUC's advice and cooperation, the TUC has only limited power to speak authoritatively for its member unions. It can act with only as much authority as its members will give it, and since there are 170 member unions, consensus is often impossible to achieve—especially when the issue is wages, which lies at the very heart of the purpose of trade unionism.

I have focused on the efforts of postwar British governments of both parties to enlist the *voluntary* cooperation of the trade union movement—through its spokesman the Trades Union Congress—in restraining the rise of wages. My purpose has been to illuminate the TUC's role in the economic policy formation process and examine the utility of Professor Beer's conception of it as a major spokesman pressure group in the "collectivist" era of British politics. It is therefore helpful to reveal what influence the behavior of the TUC and the trade union movement have had on

---

5. *Modern British Politics,* pp. 211, 318–319, 395.
6. Ibid, p. 395.

shaping the course of this frustrating and disappointing time
in Britain's economic history. I also hope that this examination offers some clues to the course and probable success of
government's management of the economy in the future.
Between 1945 and 1967 government urgently sought
the cooperation of the TUC in restraining or halting wage
inflation on four distinct occasions: 1947–1948; 1956; 1961–
1962; and 1964–1967. In all four periods government took
the initiative for wage restraint or freeze as a central part
of its efforts to relieve the serious economic crises that had
followed especially large balance of payments deficits. The
last two periods, both in the decade of the sixties, were also
intimately linked to government's efforts to move beyond
responding just to the crisis of the moment, and to combine
immediate remedial incomes policy with efforts to develop a
mechanism for effective economic planning that could work
to solve the fundamental problems that bedevil the British
economy.

Looking simply at outcomes, the relationship between
the TUC and government in the postwar years has been
uneven, despite the notably similar demands that each government (both Labour and Conservative) has made for wage
restraint or freeze. The TUC has reached agreements on
incomes policy with Labour governments but not with Conservative governments. Traditional loyalties as well as traditional animosities, rooted in continuing disagreements between the parties over the purposes of government and the
distribution of power, exercise an important influence on
the course of trade unionism's participation in modern "collectivist" politics.[7] The Attlee Labour Government in 1948
succeeded in winning the cooperation of the TUC for a
wages freeze and the TUC in turn effectively held the freeze
for more than two years. In contrast, Conservative governments in 1956 and in 1961–1962 were unable to convince
the TUC to accept any form of wage restraint. Finally, in
1964 and 1965, Wilson's Labour government succeeded in
getting the TUC to "go along" with the development of an

7. Ibid., pp. 406–407.

incomes policy that was tied to comprehensive efforts to "plan" for economic growth. However, in comparison, to the period of the Attlee government, the General Council—the TUC's directing committee of union leaders—in 1964, 1965, and 1966 was unable to implement its agreement; and wage inflation continued unchecked until the government legislated a wages freeze in 1966.

This brief review suggests also, however, a pattern of increasing paralysis for economic policy. The TUC's implementation of a severe wages freeze in 1948 demonstrated that the TUC's General Council commanded sufficient authority to translate its agreement into an effective and useful policy, i.e., to make producer group politics work. In contrast, however, the TUC was not able to implement its agreements with the Wilson government in 1964 and 1965, although they called for a significantly milder form of wage restraint. Potent opposition by the leadership of some of the largest constituent unions and by the rank and file sabotaged the agreements. This suggests that, as compared to 1948, the rationalization and convergence of the public policies of both parties has seriously eroded the authority of the General Council. For example, full employment sponsored by both parties created during the sixties a growing opposition within the trade union movement to agreements with government that compromised the unfettered pursuit of the higher wages that full employment promises. Thus, the satisfaction of specific trade union interests, rather than the force of traditional loyalties has apparently become the predominating influence in determining whether the trade union movement chooses "collaboration or conflict" with a Labour government. As for its relationship with the Conservatives, the continuation of traditional hostility and distrust has made it easy for the TUC to cite its unwillingness to compromise trade union interests as the reasons for their refusal to cooperate with Conservative governments on any proposal for wage restraint.

The chances have therefore apparently diminished that the TUC will be willing or able to cooperate with the govern-

ments of either party on such issues as incomes policy—issues
that impinge vitally on sensitive trade union interests. At the
same time, however, governments of both parties need even
greater measures of cooperation in order to "plan" for economic growth, particularly as Britain joins the European
Economic Community in 1973. This points up Beer's warning that the immobilization of policy under the weight of
"pluralistic stagnation" is a most dangerous, unintended consequence of the rise of producer group politics. Effective producer group politics depends on governments' and producer
groups' being able to reach agreements and then on each
group's being able and willing to implement its part of the
bargain. However, the indications are that the rationalization and convergence of public policies by the two major parties, recently extended by their common development of economic planning, are conspiring to paralyze economic policy
as it depends on the advice and cooperation of the TUC.

Toward a Trade Union Center and Economic Planning, 1914–1938

THE behavior of the Trades Union Congress in the postwar era of collectivist politics owes much to the course of the TUC's development during the years between the beginning of the First World War and the end of the Second. The main strands of that development were the enormous growth of the TUC before 1938 into a position as the center of the trade union movement, and then its intimate participation in economic decision making during the Second World War. Together with the new social and economic contract, these changes legitimized the postwar role of the TUC as a major spokesman producer group from whom government sought advice and cooperation for its economic policies.

At the same time, however, the TUC's role was also seriously flawed. Following the failure of the General Strike in 1926, the decision by the constituent unions to deny the General Council directing authority on any matter that touched their specific interests severely limited TUC power. The consequences of this fundamental weakness often put into jeopardy the contemporary conduct of effective economic policy.

TOWARD A TRADE UNION CENTER

The First World War was the most important stimulus for the development of the TUC into the center of British trade unionism. Although the TUC had been established in 1868, the main focus of union activity before 1914 was at the plant level. The TUC therefore functioned infrequently, "existing" only during annual congresses and occasional meetings of the Parliamentary Committee. The only full-time staff in 1914 was a single clerk.

The motive for change was the gradual extension of government control over the economy during the First World War. Increasingly, major labor problems became national in scope and their solutions depended on the development of an effective and continuous relationship between the government and a national trade union center. For example, government controls on wages and prices during the war became a dominating factor in negotiations between unions and private employers. In those industries where government took full control, as it did the railroads, mines, and shipyards in 1917, government assumed the role of the employer. When the war ended, the Lloyd George government quickly discovered that wartime interventionism had so changed economic relationships that it could not simply return to the sidelines and reestablish the unfettered primacy of private industrial relationships in the way it had hoped.[1] Concurrently, government's intervention in the economy during the war had also created a permanent need for a far stronger trade union center capable of effectively dealing with government.

The development of a stronger TUC to act as a trade union center, however, was slower and more painful than the external situation dictated. Union leaders were unprepared to deal with the new economic situation that the war posed. They initially lent their complete and unquestioning support to the war effort. Thirty-six unions voluntarily signed the Treasury Agreement during March, 1915, in which they gave up the right to strike for the duration of the war, agreed to submit unresolved disputes to binding arbi-

---

1. The most dramatic change was in the extent of industrial concentration that took place both within whole industries and correspondingly in the trade unions. This was particularly evident in the larger numbers of workers involved in each industrial dispute after the war. Cole, *An Introduction to Trade Unionism*, p. 91; and Butler and Freeman, *British Political Facts 1900–1967*, p. 219.

tration, and accepted labor dilution (the use of semiskilled and unskilled labor in skilled jobs). Congress overwhelmingly endorsed this action at its annual meeting in September, 1915.

The rank and file grumbled little about this until the end of 1915. Then, shop stewards, reflecting the growing impatience of their men, began to complain that national union leaders were ignoring the bargaining advantages that labor shortages presented. In 1916 and 1917, demand-inflation pushed prices ever higher, while incomes rose much more slowly.[2] While national union leaders continued to refuse to press the government for a more liberal wages policy, shop stewards called unofficial (wildcat) strikes to enforce their demands. In 1915 2.9 million working days were lost to strikes.[3] By 1917 the number of working days lost to strikes had jumped to 5.6 million.

The Coalition government, alarmed at this growing industrial unrest, and mindful of the Bolshevik Revolution in Russia, acted in 1917 to satisfy many of the shop stewards' demands. It relaxed the arbitration procedures to allow for more liberal wage increases, moved to restrain food prices, and appointed several union leaders, such as J. R. Clynes as Food Controller, to important administrative positions in the government. This helped to ameliorate the situation for the duration of the war. However, these actions clearly were victories for the rank and file and their shop stewards at the direct expense of their national union leadership.

The rebellion by the shop stewards occurred and was successful because the national leaders were reluctant to press the government. To reassert their authority after the war, national leaders initially concentrated on reestablishing power within their own unions by exploiting the continued economic boom. With feelings of economic and social deprivation on the rise among their members, union leaders framed their bargaining demands in the most militant terms,

2. Labour Research Department, *Wages, Prices, and Profits*, p. 109; and United States Department of Commerce, *British Wages*, p. 52.
3. Butler and Freeman, loc. cit.

and backed them up with the liberal use of the strike weapon.[4] The number of strikes in 1919 was twice that of 1917, previously considered a very bad year. Even more importantly, six times as many workers were involved in the strikes of 1919 as compared to 1917.[5] At first, it seemed that the wave of strikes had been quite successful. During 1918 and 1919 a number of wage agreements had been negotiated that provided for large increases and shorter hours. However, most of the major and long-standing grievances of the working class went unsatisfied, including complaints about exceedingly poor working conditions, the lack of social benefits, and demands for the "rationalization of production." For example, the struggle for the nationalization of the coal mines failed in 1919, and no effort was made to win workers' control of industry. Also, the large wage increases gained in 1918 and 1919 proved to be almost illusory as inflation dissipated them in 1920. Finally, the use of the strike itself produced increasingly negative consequences: war production and government control over whole industries had greatly accelerated the process of industrial concentration. This meant that labor negotiations and strikes had much wider impact. National strikes not only affected the workers whose unions were involved, but they also came to affect, as severely, workers in related activities who were not party to the dispute but nevertheless were often laid off their jobs.

These developments presented a compelling rationale for a trade union center that would be able to coordinate industrial action by the separate unions in order to maximize strike effectiveness and minimize economic dislocations. Lovell and Roberts point specifically to the railway strike of 1919 which had enormous implications for the economy and for virtually every national union, as the key factor that "led directly to an attempt to invest in the T.U.C. the power to coordinate industrial actions."[6] They conclude that "In the last analysis therefore it was the implications of the large

---

4. Runciman, *Relative Deprivation and Social Justice*, p. 59.
5. Butler and Freeman, loc. cit.
6. *A Short History of the T.U.C.*, p. 65.

scale strike which provided the *immediate* incentive to develop the T.U.C. as an authoritative trade union centre."[7]

REORGANIZATION OF THE TUC

The Transport Workers, eager to relieve the pressure on its own membership, established a mediation committee to intervene in the 1919 railroad strike.[8] The committee was so successful in settling the strike that Ernest Bevin, General Secretary of the Transport Workers, proposed the creation of permanent machinery for coordinating and mediating industrial actions. The Parliamentary Committee of the TUC subsequently appointed a Coordination Committee to study the possibility.

The Coordination Committee completed its work during 1920, and Congress accepted its recommendations at its annual meeting in September of that year. The committee's major recommendation called for the Parliamentary Committee to be enlarged and made more representative and for it to be renamed the General Council. The new General Council was authorized to hire a full-time staff to handle an expanded range of functions: to help coordinate industrial actions of all kinds; to help settle inter-union disputes; to speak for the industrial side of the labor movement in general; and to be responsible for relations with international trade unionism.

These changes created the form of a strong trade union center. The General Council held an impressive list of responsibilities and an organizational structure that seemed to make it possible for the TUC to direct effectively the trade union movement. However, in fact, the constituent unions continued to deny the TUC sufficient authority to give coherence and force to its leadership. The General Council, as the Parliamentary Committee before it, had only the power to persuade. The trade union leaders on the General

---

7. Ibid.
8. Bullock, *The Life and Times of Ernest Bevin*, p. 108.

Council, as continues to be true, primarily represented their own unions. They jealously guarded their unions' prerogatives and were most reluctant to surrender portions of their authority to the collective, i.e., the TUC. Only when they concluded that collective action would either enhance or protect their personal or individual union's interests were they willing to authorize increases in the authority of the TUC. This lack of coherence remains the fundamental weakness of the TUC.

RECESSION

Ironically, the reorganization of the TUC was not accomplished until the recession of 1921 had dissipated the widespread industrial unrest of the postwar boom period. The most serious problems were in the highly important export industries where Britain had lost a large percentage of its overseas markets to nonbelligerent countries during the war. After the war, a serious domestic inflation that made British products competitively too expensive, inhibited the effort to recapture these markets. Lower export prices would have been a large part of the solution. But since each successive government was firmly committed to regaining Britain's financial preeminence, devaluation, as the fastest and most efficient means of accomplishing lower prices, was ruled out. This meant that some way had to be found to lower production costs, the largest part of which were wage costs.

Accordingly, business began to reduce wages as unemployment soared to more than 2 million during 1921. Badly weakened by unemployment and a corresponding decline in union membership, the unions found the possibilities for successful industrial action sharply reduced. In frustration union leaders in 1922 began to depend more on the help of their Labour party allies.

The reorganization of the TUC in 1921 had been accompanied by the fashioning of a new relationship between the TUC and the Labour party. The major change was the explicit division of functions between the two wings of the labor movement. The TUC was confirmed as the leader of the industrial side and the party confirmed as the leader of the political, based on a socialist philosophy expressed in the 1918 Party *Constitution* and its accompanying manifesto, *Labour and the New Social Order.* The instrument for coordination between the two sides was the National Joint Council, created by the 1921 reorganization and on which the General Council and the Labour party Executive each held half the seats. The TUC and the Labour party further agreed to cooperate in establishing joint departments for research, public relations, and international affairs.

By these changes the TUC explicitly accepted the Labour party as the main protector of its political interests. Therefore, when Labour formed a minority government after the election of 1923, TUC leaders were quite hopeful about the prospects for solving the problems of the recession, and as a by-product, regaining the strength of the industrial movement. The actual relationship between the General Council and the brief (nine-month) MacDonald government proved, however, to be a disaster from the union's point of view. Not only did the minority character of the government make it impossible for Labour to introduce "socialist" reforms, but MacDonald and his colleagues administered a disappointingly orthodox economic policy that permitted continued high unemployment without reference to the views of the individual unions or the TUC.

The failure of the Labour government to give sympathetic attention to the unions, or to do anything significant to solve the problems of the recession reverberated strongly within the TUC.[9] Such radical leaders as Arthur Cook of the Miners and Alonzo Swales of the Engineering Union, who had rejected collaboration with Labour as the primary union strategy and had called instead for the use of direct industrial

---

9. Trades Union Congress, *Report of Proceedings, Annual Trades Union Congress* (1924), pp. 111–112.

power, gained a majority on the General Council in 1924. This led within a year and a half to a test of their philosophy in the confrontation of the 1926 General Strike.

THE GENERAL STRIKE

The details of the General Strike are well documented elsewhere.[10] The strike, particularly its failure, was significant in the development of the TUC because both radical and moderate elements came to agree (1) that the TUC should not have strong, formal power to dictate to its constituent unions, but instead should continue to depend upon the individual unions' willingness to cooperate on each issue, and (2) that trade unionism should avoid the use of direct industrial confrontation in the future, and instead should work through the political system to effect change.

Briefly, the central dispute was between the Miners Federation and the coal mine owners, over the owners' proposal to terminate the National Wages Agreement and substitute a new agreement providing for large pay cuts and longer hours. At the end of June, 1925, the owners backed up their demand by announcing that a lockout would begin on July 30 if a new agreement was not reached by that time. The Miners, for their part, replied they would call a national coal strike to resist the demand. At the same time they appealed to the TUC for help.

The General Council had been endowed by the militant-dominated 1924 Congress with stronger powers to organize and direct sympathetic union action in support of a member union's strike.[11] The General Council invoked this new power when it agreed to help. Initially, the Miners' position

---

10. See especially, Bullock, I, 279–371; and Crook, *The General Strike.*
11. "Where the Council intervenes, as before provided, and the union or unions concerned accept the assistance and advice of the Council, and where, despite the efforts of the Council, the policy of the employers enforces a stoppage of work by strike or lockout, the Council shall forthwith take steps to organize on behalf of the union or unions concerned all such moral and material support as the circumstances of the dispute may appear to justify." Trades Union Congress (1924), p. 504.

created broad sympathy and support. The mining industry had been sorely hurt by the loss of export markets and suffered from low productivity; and production was not increasing because many old mines were nearly worked out. Moreover, the industry had not experienced either a wartime or postwar prosperity and the mine workers had therefore not shared in the wage increases won in other industries, albeit temporarily, during 1918 and 1919. Some feelings of guilt existed also within the trade union movement about earlier reluctance to help the Miners, especially in their drive to have the mines nationalized. This time the General Council responded positively, and appointed a committee to develop a plan for a coal transportation embargo in the event the lockout and strike took place. At the last minute, however, the Baldwin government intervened to head off the crisis by agreeing to provide a subsidy for the industry until May 1, 1926. It appointed a Royal Commission under the chairmanship of Sir Herbert Samuel to study the problems in the industry and to make recommendations for a settlement.

A serious split began to develop within the General Council during the early spring of 1926. Moderate leaders such as J. H. Thomas of the Railwaymen became impatient with the stubborn refusal of the Miners to compromise their position even though it was increasingly apparent from the tone of the Coal Commission's inquiry that the Miners would not get most of what they wanted. Many leaders, especially Walter Citrine, the new General Secretary of the TUC, also began to worry that the movement had not made adequate preparations for a major national strike, which seemed to him to be inevitable.

The Coal Commission issued its report in March, 1926. Although the commission recommended that the coal industry be thoroughly reorganized and modernized, it called for a permanent and speedy end to the subsidy in the interim. This was clearly unacceptable to the Miners because the end to the subsidy meant that wage reductions would surely follow. The General Council on April 14, therefore, somewhat reluctantly, voted to reaffirm its support for the

Miners' strike. At the same time, however, the council
launched what proved to be futile last-ditch efforts to medi-
ate the dispute with the government.

When these efforts failed, largely due to intransigence
on both sides, a Special Conference of Union Executives
voted on May 1 to implement the General Council's strike
plan in support of the Miners. The Miners began their
strike on the same day in reaction to the owners' lockout; the
General Strike began on May 4. Logistically, the General
Council carried off the strike quite smoothly, and the men
responded with enthusiasm and unity. About 1.25 million
workers went on strike, primarily in the transport, iron and
steel, printing, gas, and electricity industries. But the government had prepared well in the ten months since the previous
crisis, and easily maintained the flow of essential goods and
services. Within a few days, it became obvious to many on
the General Council that the strike could not succeed. Their
gloom was reinforced by the Miners' refusal to accept the
General Council's primacy in negotiations or to soften their
position, and in their failure to convince the government to
give at least token assurances that remedial action would be
taken in the mine workers' behalf if they returned to work.
On May 12 the General Council dramatically called off the
strike, without having won any of the strike's objectives.[12]
The Miners were left to continue their strike, without success, until the autumn.

With the aid of hindsight, the strike appears to have
been far more successful than it first seemed. At the very
least it dissuaded employers in other industries from trying
to exert the same kind of overt pressure on wages. In the
long run, the strike was an important and impressive display
of trade union power that forced business and government to
treat trade unionism with considerably more deference. At
that moment, however, the failure of the General Strike sent
a shock wave through the movement. The defeat reflected
most strongly on the General Council, and specifically on the

12. *The British Worker* (London), May 12, 1926, pp. 1–2.

leadership that fostered the policy of massive industrial confrontation during 1924 and 1925. The General Council called a Conference of Union Executives in January, 1927, to hold an inquest into the strike.

The conference did not reach any important conclusions about the strike or provide the movement with new directions. Rather, the conference's most important action was to accept the General Council's report on the strike, which implicitly confirmed the positions of Walter Citrine and Ernest Bevin and their more moderate colleagues as the dominating personalities and leaders of the poststrike movement. Both men had been active leaders in the strike, although they had become openly critical of the Miners' stubbornness and had generally questioned the value of massive industrial action.[13] Additionally, Citrine at the conference had turned away criticism of the General Council by charging that the real problem was that unions throughout the movement were illy prepared intellectually or organizationally to accept central direction.[14]

Over the next six years, Bevin and Citrine, working in conjunction with such other moderate leaders as J. H. Thomas, Arthur Pugh, and W. Milne-Bailey of the TUC Research Department, redefined the goals and revised the strategy of the TUC. Citrine stated its approach and defined his close collaboration with Bevin quite succinctly in his autobiography, *Men and Work:*

The principal lesson I had learned was that the trade union movement must exert its influence in an ever-widening sphere and not be contained within the traditional walls of trade union policy. Events were moving fast and the widely held belief in the impending collapse of capitalism would not suffice. We must try to expand the activities of the T.U.C. until we could establish an efficient system whereby the T.U.C. would be regularly and naturally consulted by whatever Government was in power on any subject of direct concern to the unions. I reasoned that this was a policy to be advocated whenever I got the chance. So, almost

13. Bullock, I, 306.
14. Citrine, *Men and Work,* p. 217.

without realizing it, I found myself evolving a twofold policy, the parts of which were interdependent. The first led towards more power to the T.U.C., and the second was a demand for consultation in the widest area of economic and industrial policy.

.   .   .   .

It was here that the remarkable relationship of Ernest Bevin and I had scope for development. Our ideas were so closely related, our thinking so closely parallel, that without any formal collaboration we reached similar conclusions. . . .[15]

The Citrine-Bevin approach was pragmatic. The authority of the General Council was under serious attack from within the movement, and trade union prestige and influence on business and government was at a very low level. Socialism would continue to be the long-term goal, but the TUC had to do the best with the situation at hand if it was to serve its constituent members effectively. This meant that the TUC would have to develop its own capability to understand and express its views on current industrial, economic, social, and political problems, with the purpose of carving out trade unionism's place in the capitalist system's decision-making process.[16]

They also sought to overcome the view formed by both moderate and radical elements in the wake of the failure of the General Strike that the TUC should not be endowed with strong, decisive authority to order direct industrial action or otherwise dictate to its constituent members.[17] The moderate leaders very much feared that a strong TUC with dictatorial powers would always be open to control again by radical factions that might launch further disastrous "adventures." Radical leaders, on the other hand, worried that the "sellout" of the miners demonstrated that a powerful General Council, dominated by moderates, would compromise the interests of individual unions still further. They felt that it would be better to retain their own authority than depend on weak, uncertain, and often hostile assistance.

The notion that the TUC should depend ultimately on

---

15. P. 238.
16. Bullock, I, 393.
17. Lovell and Roberts, "A Short History of the T.U.C.," pp. 95–96.

the voluntary cooperation of its constituent unions has remained operative and at issue up to the present. Yet, without strong formal authority, the TUC has carved out its role and influence on economic policy largely in response to the demands that government has made for its cooperation, and correspondingly on how those demands and the demands of "the times" have created a need in the constituent unions for the help and "protection" of the TUC. Further, the power and authority of the TUC has been closely related to the forcefulness and ideas of its leadership. In this period, Citrine and Bevin provided exceptionally strong leadership that launched the TUC on its quest for access and influence within the context of the existing economic and political system.

Mond-Turner

The first substantive implementation of the Citrine-Bevin philosophy was the Mond-Turner discussions of 1928 and 1929. Sir Alfred Mond, Chairman of Imperial Chemicals, headed a group of business executives interested in establishing a dialogue with the trade unions on the economic and industrial problems facing both sides of business in the wake of the General Strike. Responding to discussions at the 1927 Congress about expanding contacts with business, Mond invited the General Council to a wide-ranging series of talks. The General Council, headed by Ben Turner, agreed, making the decision over the objections of more radical trade union leaders who charged that such talks would be a surrender of union ambitions for the radical transformation of society in favor of a wholesale collaboration with capitalism.

These talks began in January, 1928. They proved to be extremely useful in broadening the General Council's understanding of a wide range of industrial and economic issues that went far beyond the more traditional trade union concern with wages, hours, and working conditions. Collaborating with its newly established Research Department, the

General Council for the first time sought to develop its views on the larger issues of monetary, fiscal, and general economic policy, including the crucially important problem of unemployment. In July, 1928, the two sides issued an Interim Report.[18] Their major proposal was to establish a National Industrial Council to provide a continuous forum for discussions of common industrial problems by representatives of the TUC and the two major employers' groups, the National Confederation of Employers' Organizations (NCEO) and the Federation of British Industries (FBI).

The next step, to initiate discussions with the NCEO and the FBI on the basis of the Mond-Turner recommendations, proved far more difficult. Suspicious of trade unionism, both groups initially rejected any form of consultation, especially on the basis of the Mond-Turner recommendations. After some hesitation, however, they reversed themselves in part and agreed to hold separate consultations with the TUC so long as the agenda was not prescribed in advance. The FBI subsequently initiated talks in February, 1930, on the question of developing evidence for the Macmillan committee then conducting an inquiry into British monetary policy, and on the possibilities of developing a joint policy towards Commonwealth affairs.

These talks were not especially fruitful and ended during 1931 because the problems of the depression tended to harden positions on both sides. However, the talks were extremely useful as an opening wedge. The reasonable and constructive proposals put forward by the General Council surprised the employers' side. When Britain faced the problems of rearmament eight years later, the employers' associations readily renewed consultations with the TUC that then set an important pattern for post-Second World War industrial relations.

THE SECOND LABOUR GOVERNMENT

While the General Council held discussions with first the Mond group and then the FBI during 1929 and 1930, the

18. Trades Union Congress, *Report of Proceedings, Annual Trades Union Congress* (1928), pp. 219–230.

TUC pursued its parallel aim of establishing regular consultations with the government-of-the-day. Relations with the Baldwin government were very poor, especially after the Tories passed the Trade Disputes Act in 1927 that outlawed sympathetic strikes, abolished "contracting out" of the union levy for the Labour party,[19] and forbade civil servants from holding memberships in unions that were members of the TUC. The General Council, however, was encouraged when Labour formed its Second government in 1929.[20] Tensions between the party and the TUC had persisted throughout the decade and the General Council distrusted Ramsay Mac-Donald and still indirectly blamed him for not acting to mitigate the circumstances that eventually led to the General Strike. But the TUC-Labour alliance remained workable because there continued to be an overriding sense of class identity and agreement about economic and social goals, as well as an interlocking organizational machinery that maintained contact between the leadership. The General Council was hopeful it would receive a better hearing from this government than it had five years earlier by presenting its own well-defined positions on important issues with which it was especially concerned.

The deepening recession, however, upset these plans. Although the Labour government and the TUC agreed about the long-term goals of socialization, they disagreed

---

19. "In the early days of the Labour movement many of the trade unions used part of the regular dues collected from their members for political purposes, aiding the Labour Representation Committee and sometimes supporting members of Parliament. In 1909, however, a court decision, the Osborne Judgment, declared that money collected for ordinary trade union purposes could not be spent on political objectives. This decision threatened to curtail seriously the political activities of the unions and indirectly to thwart the growth of the Labour movement. Relief came four years later when Parliament authorized the trade unions to establish political funds and to collect assessments from all their members who did not 'contract out' of payment. The Trade Disputes Act, 1927, following the general strike of 1926, amended the law concerning political contributions by limiting the assessment to those trade union members who affirmatively approved, that is, who 'contracted in.' A repeal of the Trade Disputes Act was one of the first things done by the Labour Government when it came into office in 1945, and thus the situation with respect to the political funds of the trade unions was restored to its pre-1927 status." Hiram M. Stout, *British Government*, pp. 198–199.
20. Cole, *A History of the Labour Party from 1914*, p. 229.

sharply about how to treat the immediate problems of unemployment and financial collapse. The fact that the TUC
had done its own thinking and reached its own conclusions
sharpened the disagreements. The government, as in 1924,
stuck to a rather orthodox approach that emphasized putting
its own economic house in order by cutting expenditures and
balancing the budget. The General Council, using the work
of its own Research Department, emphasized the Keynesian
analysis of the growing depression and strongly urged greatly
increased government spending, even if that meant large
budgetary deficits, in order to generate increased consumer
demand.[21]

Now, as in the years to follow, the TUC's economic
staff enthusiastically promoted an expansionist approach to
economic policy, with the consistent and virtually unanimous
approval of the General Council. The council supported
progressive economic thinking that emphasized high employment and increased government spending because both
would be clearly in the union interest, and, the council believed, in the national interest as well.

The dispute between the government and the TUC
simmered from issue to issue during 1930. It reached a climax in 1931 when the depression began to have a distinctly
erosive effect on the government's political support. As it
came under increasing partisan attack for its handling of the
depression, the government resorted to its store of political
friends, among whom the trade unions were probably its
most important. This action gave the General Council an
important influence on the government's continued viability.
The TUC used this leverage in the spring of 1931 to dissuade
MacDonald from implementing the Macmillan Committee's
recommendation for a cut in unemployment compensation.[22]
But in August a European banking crisis seemingly put the
international financial structure in danger of collapse.
Alarmed, MacDonald and Philip Snowden prepared a plan

21. Trades Union Congress, *Report of Proceedings, Annual Trades Union
Congress* (1931), p. 261.
22. Cole, *History of the Labour Party*, loc. cit.

for severe deflation in order to restore the country's fiscal integrity, and requested the General Council to lend its support. The General Council refused, and, as Pelling comments,

. . . [T] he General Council's opposition at once strengthened the will of Henderson and other Cabinet Ministers who had been doubtful of Snowden's policy; and it became clear to MacDonald that he could not carry his proposals without a serious Cabinet split. He therefore resigned office on August 23rd. . . .[23]

The General Council had not been very successful in positively influencing the government to accept its views on economic policy. It was, however, quite negatively influential as the Second Labour government lost political strength. Ironically, the exercise of that negative power in August, 1931, contributed to an almost complete loss of influence, negative or positive, on the succeeding government.

Toward Economic Planning

The Labour government was succeeded in 1931 by a MacDonald-led and Tory-dominated National Government that was little concerned with the economic views of the trade union movement. For their part, members of the General Council distrusted and disliked the Tories, and this was compounded by their personal bitterness toward MacDonald, Snowden, and the others who had broken with the Labour party to participate in the new government.[24]

The ebbing of TUC influence on the immediate problems generated by the depression impelled a shift in the General Council's concerns. Specifically, the General Council began to explore the larger questions of how the economy

23. *A History of British Trade Unionism,* p. 195.
24. Citrine, p. 287.

could be ordered so that the workingman could be protected from the ravages of future recessions and depressions. The Labour party had done the spadework on these questions in 1918 when it issued *Labour and the New Social Order,* and trade unionism supported these views. The details, however, particularly as they related to the union movement, had never been spelled out. There was a growing feeling that the movement would be in a position to protect its members adequately only when the TUC had achieved a legitimate and institutionalized role in a *new* economic context.

The first efforts in this direction were undertaken by the TUC in early 1931. Sharp disagreements between the TUC and the Labour party (described above) led the TUC Economic Committee to authorize a study of the depression by its Research Department. The immediate purpose of this work was to prepare specific short-term economic policy proposals for Congress's approval, that could then be presented to the government with the full force of the movement behind them.

The work of the Research Department went more slowly than expected, and the report was not ready for the 1931 Congress. By the time that Congress convened in September, the Labour government had already resigned. Since the chances of dealing with the National Government were poor, Congress changed the instructions for the Research Department. The new instructions greatly expanded the scope of the study. In part, they were contained in a resolution submitted on behalf of the General Council by Arthur Pugh to the 1931 Congress stating the council's interest in the concept of economic planning:

> This Congress, being in accord with the traditional policy of the Trade Union Movement, welcomes the present tendency towards a planned and regulated economy in our national life.

> Having regard to the seriousness of the economic situation, Congress expresses the view that only by a comprehensive planning of our economic development and regulated trading relations can the needs of the present day be met.

> Congress therefore instructs the General Council to advance

this policy both nationally and internationally, keeping in mind
that in order to maintain and improve the standard of living, the
people as consumers must be protected by public control and reg-
ulation from exploitation.[25]

The Research Department, headed by W. Milne-Bailey,
approached its expanded assignment influenced primarily by
two streams of thought. The first was the general concept of
socialism endorsed by the labor movement when it accepted
the 1918 Labour party *Constitution* and supported the manifesto, *Labour and the New Social Order*. The other was the
thinking of John Maynard Keynes about the causes and
remedies for the world depression that he later synthesized in
his *General Theory*.[26]

Socialist ideology was appealing because of the trade
unionists' feelings of class deprivation. There was the attrac-
tion of the good life in the utopian society where every individual would have a relatively equal chance to develop his
capabilities through his commitment to the communal purpose. Specifically, socialism was appealing to trade unionists
in the midst of the depression, because, as Wertheimer comments, British socialism uniquely (as compared to "socialism
of the rest of the world") considers its main task the

radical change in the distribution of incomes . . . by the
transfer of the means of production to the ownership and control
of the community . . . within the framework of the capitalist
machine.[27]

Clause 4 of the 1918 Labour party *Constitution* was thus
particularly relevant: socialism would:

. . . secure for the producers by hand or by brain the full
fruits of their industry, and the most equitable distribution
thereof that may be possible, upon the basis of the common ownership of the means of production and the best obtainable system

---

25. Trades Union Congress (1931), p. 406.
26. *The End of Laissez-Faire;* and *The General Theory of Employment, Interest and Money* (New York: Harcourt, Brace, 1936). Keynes also wrote fre-
quent articles for *New Statesman and Nation*.
27. Wertheimer, "Portrait of the Labour Party," p. 34.

of popular administration and control of each industry and service.[28]

Keynes, on the other hand, emphasized the responsibilities of an activist government for maintaining employment levels at the highest possible point. Orthodox economics was turned on its head. Economists had been wrong, Keynes said, in assuming that the downward swing of the business cycle would be accompanied by a fall in interest rates that would at a certain point, and by itself, generate renewed inflows of investment capital and trigger an upswing. In the explanation of his equilibrium concept, Keynes showed that the depression could go on indefinitely until some action was taken to break the equilibrium. Most interesting and appealing for trade unionists, responsibility for the persistence of bad times was placed on the government. Government, from Keynes's point of view, had the power and the responsibility for taking actions that would increase effective demand to the point that full employment would be reestablished and prosperity rebuilt.

In its work, the Research Department attempted to synthesize these two streams of thought. Keynes's concept of an active and responsible government was blended with the socialist idea of public ownership of the means of production for the common good. The product of this synthesis was contained in the 1932 TUC Economic Report.

THE 1932 REPORT

The report, *Trade Unionism and the Control of Industry,* was endorsed by the General Council and submitted to Congress in September, 1932. Its main theme was the movement toward ". . . government interference with the uncontrolled conduct of economic affairs."[29] Many of the delegates to Congress objected, however, to the mild, almost conservative, tone of a number of the specific proposals:

28. Labour Party, *Constitution,* clause 4, p. 4.
29. Trades Union Congress, *Report of Proceedings, Annual Trades Union Congress* (1932), p. 207.

A. The report rejected the ". . . more ideal programme . . ." of the complete socialization of the economy and the consequent elimination of private enterprise.[30] Although the report supported the replacement of the profit motive, it said that only some industries were ready for socialization. These (to be identified in later reports), along with services that related to the life and safety of the community, would become publicly controlled. The others would be left under private control, either to be regulated by the government or left completely alone.

B. The long-cherished trade union dream of workers' control was also rejected. The report, instead, endorsed the principle of expert management that would be free from political pressure. Also, socialized industries should be established as public corporations and not be run by government departments. Each public corporation would have a Board of Management consisting of persons appointed by the government solely on merit, not excluding any class but not selecting any members as representatives of particular interests. Functional representation would be limited to advisory committees for each industry.

C. On the national level, the report revived the recommendation produced by the Mond-Turner talks for the establishment of a National Joint Council.

The most intense opposition to the report at Congress was focused on the question of workers' control. The heat generated by that issue tended to obscure the General Council's purpose. C. T. Cramp, speaking for the General Council in the debate, tried to emphasize the purpose of the report, and to relate it to the term "economic planning":

The term "planning" is now fashionable, but the principle it stands for is as old as Socialism itself, and is not an invention of Soviet Russia. In the case mention of Russia suggests one particular type of social and economic planning we must make it clear to everyone that the methods which Russia or any other country may think best adopted to its own peculiar circumstances cannot be the most suitable for this country, with its different history and

30. Ibid., p. 206.

different conditions. Nor by planning do we mean a detailed su-
pervision and regimentation all through the economic system.
We mean rather that continuous progress should be made towards the intelligent organization of production, distribution
and finance in the interests of the whole community.[31]

What the General Council attempted to do in this report
was consistent with Citrine-Bevin pragmatism. The council,
through its Economic Committee, enunciated a set of specific
trade union aspirations that it hoped to have accepted in
workable terms. The report, in essence, proposed the reorganization of industry along lines that would greatly increase
government's responsibilities and participation in the economy. These changes would necessitate new forms of economic
decision making at the local, industry, and national levels
and, the council hoped, would institutionalize and legitimize
trade union participation at all points. The term economic
planning was arbitrarily used by the General Council to denote, in effect, its own plan for industrial reorganization.

This report also implied significant changes in the distribution of power within the trade union movement. Historically, power flowed from the local level through the national unions and from there to the TUC. Nationalization,
a National Industrial Council, and the other suggested
changes would increase the decision-making responsibilities
of the national unions and the TUC at the expense of local
union organizations. The report therefore raised questions
(which were to become relevant in the postwar years) about
whether the local unions would be willing to defer to their
leadership in London, and, if they would not, whether
stronger government intervention in the economy in the
context of economic planning could be successful.

ALLIANCE WITH THE LABOUR PARTY

The 1932 report spelled out the General Council's economic aspirations. The problem was to translate them into

31. Ibid., p. 203.

reality. With this in mind, the General Council turned to trade unionism's traditional alliance with the Labour party in late 1932. Quarrels between the General Council and the party leadership had marked their relationship during the previous dozen years. They had reached a climax of bitterness and recrimination during the crisis of August, 1931, and the subsequent resignation of the Second Labour government. The quarrels, however, had been principally with the policies and personalities of MacDonald and Snowden. Now both men and their supporters had left the party, and the General Council therefore felt that this was an excellent time to renew the alliance.

The General Council knew that Labour was unlikely to regain enough parliamentary seats in the foreseeable future to have a chance to form a new government. However, as Lovell and Roberts point out, Labour's weakness gave the TUC a unique opportunity to press its views successfully on the party. The General Council viewed the reinvigoration of the alliance as a good investment even if it would not pay off for an indefinite time. For their part, the new party leadership of Arthur Henderson and then George Lansbury with his deputy Clement Attlee were eager to begin rebuilding the party's electoral strength by solidifying its basic core of trade union support.[32]

The General Council's strategy for its economic plans was twofold: first, it sought to convince the party to accept the 1932 report as the basis for developing an economic policy blueprint for the next Labour government.[33] As a corollary, it sought to bind that government to implement that blueprint.

The vehicle for the General Council's strategy was the National Joint Council, renamed the National Council of Labour in 1935.[34] Although the Joint Council had been created in 1921 under the TUC reorganization to serve as the coordinating body for the two sides of the labor movement,

---

32. Lovell and Roberts, p. 123.
33. Trades Union Congress, *The History of the T.U.C. 1868–1968*, p. 100.
34. Pelling, pp. 199–200.

it had fallen into disuse during the intervening years of friction between the General Council and the party. Following the 1931 crisis, Citrine took the initiative in reviving the Joint Council on TUC terms.

Beginning in 1932, the Joint Council became the leading spokesman for the labor movement, "functioning much as Citrine had wished."[35] Its leadership was primarily in the area of foreign affairs, especially as the international situation deteriorated after 1935. But during the worst of the depression, from 1932 to 1935, the Joint Council took an active interest in economic policy and specifically initiated the collaboration between the TUC Economic Committee and the party's Research Department on the development of a common economic policy, especially economic reorganization. Also in 1933, the Joint Council was instrumental in influencing the party Conference, still reeling from the shock of "MacDonaldism," to accept a new set of rules intended to tie future Labour governments more closely to the wishes of the party organization and membership. The party leadership was required to consult with, among other bodies, the National Joint Council before forming a government, and, once formed, to consult regularly with the Joint Council on important policy questions.

In sum, the TUC's investment in the party during the thirties proved to have been well placed, both in the short and the long term. Although most of the restraints adopted by the party in 1933 were overlooked in 1945, their essence was not lost on Attlee and his colleagues. Trade unionism was brought into close consultation with the Third Labour government. Although the Attlee government's economic program was hardly a carbon copy of the 1932 TUC report or the subsequent collaboration between the Economic Committee and the Research Department, the work of those years did form the essential framework upon which the experience of the war economy and the special needs of the postwar period were added.

---

35. Ibid.

CONCLUSION

The TUC's proposals for economic planning contained a serious contradiction. The TUC sought to develop both vigorous government management of the economy as well as to establish a place for itself at the center of economic decision making. Both assumed the TUC would be able to fulfill its commitments to take action in this new role as a participant in economic management. Yet, although the TUC had developed remarkably since the beginning of the First World War into the center of the trade union movement by 1938, it still lacked significant authority to direct and control its unions on matters that touched their specific interests. In sum, the TUC's proposals for economic planning and for assuming a role in economic decision making required a degree of authority it did not have, and, further, authority which its constituent members had specifically decided to deny it. This contradiction was important only in the abstract during the bleak days of the thirties when both the TUC and the Labour party were still far from the center of power. However, in later years, after the Second World War, the dilemma took on concrete meaning as the very hopes that Citrine and Bevin enunciated in the years after the General Strike were realized and the TUC became a crucially important spokesman group in the collectivist era of British politics.

The Transformation of
Trades Union Congress Power,
1938–1945

T HE Chamberlain government's belated decision in 1938 to begin serious preparations for war marked the beginning of the contemporary era of British trade unionism.[1] Historically, the trade union movement had been an institution for the expression of economic and social protest from a position on the fringes of power. Walter Citrine and Ernest Bevin had sought, however, to secure a place for the Trades Union Congress at the very center of national economic decision making while gaining power for the TUC within the labor movement.[2] They believed that the failure of direct industrial confrontation in the General Strike demonstrated the need for trade unionism to have a strong centralized spokesman group that could effectively seek economic change within the existing political system instead of waiting hopefully for the collapse of capitalism. By 1938, the TUC was enormously more important as the center of trade unionism than it had been before the First World War, although it sorely lacked substantial authority. It was still, however, a "voice in the wilderness."[3] Ignored by the Tory-dominated National Government and then by the two succeeding Conservative governments, the TUC had been unable to exert

---

1. The decision to launch a major rearmament program developed fitfully over several months, but the most important date seems to have been March 22, 1938, when the Cabinet ". . . took the decision to cancel the assumption on which the reconditioning of the Services had hitherto been based. . . ." See Hancock and Gowing (eds.), *British War Economy*, p. 70.
2. Citrine, *Men and Work*, p. 217.
3. Lovell and Roberts, *A Short History of the T.U.C.*, p. 144.

any influence on the course of public policy dealing with the depression.

The beginning of serious rearmament in 1938 changed everything. The problem of manpower shortages, production delays, wage inflation, and strikes compelled the Chamberlain government gradually to open relations with the unions and the TUC. The coming of war, in sum, completely reversed labor's bargaining position. The historic problem of unemployment gave way to the contemporary problem of full employment. Government began to consult with the TUC on the "widest area of economic and industrial policy."[4] In turn, the TUC faced new and unfamiliar questions about the purposes, terms, and limits of its collaboration with government. With Bevin as Minister of Labour in the Coalition government, the TUC worked hard to cement the legitimacy of its new role in economic decision making.

REARMAMENT

The growing shortage of skilled manpower in 1939 was the first specific issue on which the Chamberlain government urgently sought the TUC's cooperation. The shortages were most severe in the vital engineering and shipbuilding trades which had steadily lost manpower since the beginning of production cutbacks in 1921. The government now wanted TUC cooperation in regulating the allocation of manpower, and in putting an end to "poaching" by sorely pressed employers who were suddenly facing avalanches of orders. Although the government could have easily passed restrictive legislation without TUC approval, the Minister of Labour, Ernest Brown, was anxious to avoid provoking the TUC if he could, at so difficult a time.[5]

The first meeting between the General Council and Brown was held in July, 1939. It was brief and fruitless.

---

4. Citrine, p. 238.
5. Pelling, *A History of British Trade Unionism*, p. 215.

Both sides agreed there was need for remedial action, but the TUC vigorously insisted that the voluntary joint bargaining machinery in each industry be allowed to handle this and all labor problems during rearmament or wartime.[6] Brown curtly rejected this proposal as usurping too much of the government's power and maneuverability, and complained that it would be applicable to a small percentage only of the total work force.

The issue remained unresolved until shortly after the Germans invaded Poland on September 1. Then, pressured by the beginning of the shooting war, Brown introduced a Control of Employment Bill without consulting the TUC until just hours before he presented the bill to the House of Commons.[7]

The General Council angrily protested both the government's failure to give them reasonable notice, as well as the bill's purpose. The bill provided only for a mild form of negative labor direction: it merely prohibited employers from advertising for labor or hiring except through employment exchanges. However, this was a significant departure from the concept of complete voluntarism and the General Council was strongly opposed to any arrangement, however mild, that even hinted of infringing on the long-standing principle of voluntary arrangements between trade unions and employers.[8]

Nevertheless, the government introduced the bill as planned on September 5. Two days later, Sir Thomas Phillips, the permanent secretary to the Ministry of Labour, met with the General Council to discuss the TUC's objections. Citrine made it clear at this meeting that the TUC strongly resented the way the government had handled the bill from the beginning, and he took particular exception to Brown's assurances to the House on September 5 that he had fully consulted with the TUC.[9] He proposed that the government reconsider the bill and amend it to instruct the Minister of

6. Bullock, *The Life and Times of Ernest Bevin*, I, 642.
7. Trades Union Congress, *Report of Proceedings, Annual Trades Union Congress* (1940), pp. 166–167.
8. Ibid.; *Daily Herald* (London), September 6, 1939, p. 7.
9. Ibid.; *The Times* (London), September 6, 1939, p. 5.

Labour not "to make any Order under the Act until he had referred a draft of the Order to an advisory committee that should consist of an equal number of trade union and employers' representatives."[10]

Labour MPs strongly supported this proposal in the ensuing debate in the House of Commons. After first adamantly refusing to make any changes, the government on September 14 announced it would accept modifying amendments in order to have a workable policy in the war emergency. However, the success of the TUC efforts to modify the bill produced an act that restricted the Minister of Labour from exercising control over hiring in any industry until after he had completed a cumbersome and time-consuming series of consultations and appeals.

In the wake of the struggle over the Control of Employment Bill, the government abandoned its consultation-as-an-afterthought approach to the TUC. Instead, it soon offered the TUC full and regular consultations.

The first solid evidence that the government had decided to establish regular consultations with the labor movement came a few days after the passage of the Control of Employment Act. First, on October 4, 1939, the Minister of Labour met with both sides of industry and announced that he was immediately creating a National Joint Advisory Committee. This committee, frequently proposed by the TUC and endorsed by a Special Conference of Union Executives in May, 1939, would serve in an advisory capacity to his office and have thirty members, fifteen each nominated by both labor and management. The committee would explore any "matters in which employers and workers have a common interest."[11]

On the following day, October 5, the General Council met with Prime Minister Chamberlain to protest the government's action in setting up a Ministry of Supply without first consulting with the TUC. The Prime Minister, in the course of that meeting, asked the trade union leaders how

10. Ibid.; *Daily Herald* (London), September 7, 1939, p. 6.
11. Trades Union Congress (1940), pp. 167–168; Citrine, *Two Careers,* p. 28.

they viewed trade unionism's and specifically the TUC's role during wartime. Lord Citrine replied that although the TUC strongly supported the government's efforts to speed preparations for war, that the TUC must insist that as a condition of its collaboration, the government extend "the fullest recognition of the Trade Unions to function on [the workers'] behalf."[12]

More than a week later, at a follow-up meeting, Bullock reports that Chamberlain read Citrine his instructions that all departments consult with the TUC and individual unions on any matter that might affect them, directly or indirectly.

Thus, the General Council had won from the government, and an unfriendly Tory government at that, the comprehensive recognition it had sought from both Labour and Conservative governments since the end of the General Strike. Suspicion and distrust persisted, but both sides had agreed to recognize each other's interests in order to facilitate wartime cooperation. The TUC's price was full and regular consultations; in return it promised to cooperate on the myriad of wartime labor problems. Wages, however, were pointedly not part of this bargain. The TUC in 1939 still considered voluntary wage bargaining as inviolable.

The TUC's success in widening trade union influence with government also markedly enhanced its position within the trade union movement. Government's recognition of the TUC as the legitimate consultative and bargaining agent for the whole labor movement placed the TUC in a position to make rapid decisions on the most crucial issues without reference to a polling of constituent unions. Decisions reached in daily consultations were *faits accomplis* for the movement by the time they were perfunctorily put to Congress for ratification, often months later.[13] On the other hand, the war was an unusual time, and although the constituent unions tacitly agreed to this widening of the power of the General Council and the General Secretary, they still

---

12. Trades Union Congress (1940), p. 230.
13. TUC decisions were not usually ratified item by item by Congress, but merely as part of the General Council's lengthy *Annual Report*.

held the ultimate power to refuse to cooperate with the decisions made at the TUC. However, in the context of the war, constituent unions rarely countermanded the decisions of either Citrine or the General Council. The wartime crisis was too overwhelming.

BEVIN AND THE WAR

The German Army's rout of British forces during the spring of 1940 triggered the resignation of the Chamberlain government. Winston Churchill, who had severely criticized Chamberlain's rearmament program, became prime minister and formed a coalition explicitly pledged to begin an all-out effort to prepare the nation for war.

Churchill's most important Labour appointments were those of Clement Attlee and Arthur Greenwood to be members of the five-man Cabinet, and Ernest Bevin to be Minister of Labour and National Service. The selection of Bevin was a surprise. Bevin had never served in Parliament nor devoted very much time to politics. His appointment underscored the new prime minister's concern with the problems of manpower and industrial relations. Churchill had been impressed at the time of the General Strike with the enormous power of organized labor and he appointed Bevin explicitly as the union representative in the government, and a few months later in the Cabinet. He hoped that Bevin, the most respected and powerful personality in the trade union movement, could do more than any other person to win the TUC's confidence and cooperation for the conduct of the domestic war effort.[14]

It would be difficult to overestimate the contribution that Bevin made to solving the problems of industrial relations and manpower allocation during the war, and the effects

---

14. In his memoirs, Churchill expresses great satisfaction both with securing Bevin's consent to serve as Minister of Labour and later with Bevin's success in enlisting trade union support. See Churchill, *Their Finest Hour*, pp. 12, 112, 234–325.

that his policies had on permanently transforming the relationship of the TUC to government, business, and its own constituent members. The task before him when he took office in May, 1940, was extraordinarily difficult: he had to develop the highest possible level of productivity and output from a rapidly shrinking and increasingly unskilled labor force, and to do it as quickly as possible but without generating a serious wage inflation.

In meeting these problems, Bevin strongly impressed his own firmly held views about industrial relations on the way he conducted his office. He was convinced that compulsion was totally counterproductive in employer-employee relationships.[15] The traditional principles of voluntarism, he felt, had to be preserved. Undoubtedly, much centralized decision making would have to take place in wartime and suspicions between employer and employee were too entrenched to be swept away by government's simply issuing a directive. But the war was a unique opportunity for both sides of industry to demonstrate the effectiveness of voluntary agreement and action. For trade unionism specifically, the war was a special chance, as Citrine had said, "to widen the ambit and influence of the movement by contributing its maximum effort to the war's struggle.[16] He further agreed with Citrine that "if our Movement and our class rise with all their energy now and save the people of this country from disaster, the country will always turn with confidence to the people who saved them."[17]

Starting from these views, Bevin very quickly and decisively spelled out his policy. Labor direction, wages, conditions of work, and all other matters concerning industrial relations would be developed as much as possible through a system of tripartite negotiations between government, business, and labor. At every point, however, special attention would be paid to maintaining an "equality of sac-

15. Bullock, *The Life and Times of Ernest Bevin*, II, 45.
16. Trades Union Congress (1940), p. 229.
17. Trades Union Congress, *Report of the Special Conference of Trades Union Executives on May 25, 1940*, p. 18.

rifice"; material goods would be available to everyone according to a policy of "fair shares."

Bevin faced severe competing pressures as he moved to confirm this policy within a few days of taking office. Many members in Parliament, in both parties, wanted to legislate industrial relations questions for the duration of the war. The pressure was especially intense because the unchecked German advances through Europe were urgently raising the threat of a German attempt to invade Britain itself. On the labor side, however, the question of wages and working conditions was becoming quite volatile as employment levels began to turn upward.[18] Accordingly, most union leaders were under a good deal of pressure, as they had been in 1918, to press for wage increases. Pressure was coming most strongly from the powerful and relatively better-off craft unions whose members were already experiencing full employment. Bevin therefore sought to frame policies that struck a balance between the urgent needs of war, and the problem of preserving the ability of trade union leadership to give effect to their agreements.

Bevin's finesse in solving these problems both for the short term as well as for the duration of the war was remarkable. Parliament passed an Emergency Powers Act within a few days of Bevin's taking office that gave the Minister of Labour the unprecedented authority to direct any person to perform any job. Bevin had not asked for this authority and he did not intend to use it except under the most extreme conditions, but it gave him a good deal of leverage in working out other solutions.

On the same day, May 22, 1940, Bevin met with his National Joint Advisory Council. He proposed that the council appoint a smaller working subgroup of seven trade unionists nominated by the TUC and seven employers' rep-

18. For an analytical and historical discussion of relative deprivation among the British working classes during the depression, see Runciman, *Relative Deprivation and Social Justice*, chap. IV; as unemployment declined between 1937 and 1939, the number of work stoppages (compared with the most serious depression years, 1932–1935), sharply increased. See Butler and Freeman, *British Political Facts 1900–1967*, p. 219.

resentatives to advise the Minister of Labour on a daily basis throughout the war. The new group would be known as the Joint Consultative Committee.

Both sides agreed to the proposal and the Joint Consultative Committee met for the first time on May 28. Bevin wasted no time in posing his policy dilemma to the new group. He told them he had been considering some limited form of wage controls, but that despite the seriousness of the country's position he still preferred not to use his powers of compulsion, except where he found no alternative. He hoped both sides of industry could therefore find some other way to solve the issues of wages, strikes, lockouts, and conditions of work for the duration of the war.

Spurred by Bevin's exhortation and implied threat to take matters into his own hands, the committee was able to agree upon a proposal within two weeks. They recommended, in a report to Bevin on June 4, that wage bargaining be continued during the war. Also they proposed that strikes and lockouts be banned and that when wages and other questions were not resolved by the parties themselves, that they be submitted to binding arbitration. Bevin accepted these recommendations and on June 10 gave them the force of law, when he issued the now famous Order 1305.[19]

Sporadic and sometimes serious challenges to Order 1305 and to Bevin's approach to labor problems in general occurred throughout the war. For example, Kingsley Wood, Chancellor of the Exchequer, pressed for wage controls in the summer of 1941.[20] But Bevin held his ground and with Churchill's support preserved the spirit and purpose of voluntarism, with only minor restrictions, until the end of the war in 1945.[21]

Bevin's success in institutionalizing voluntarism and tripartite relationships in labor relations and economic de-

---

19. Lovell and Roberts, pp. 146–147. Specifically, Order 1305 created a National Arbitration Tribunal and prohibited strikes and lockouts.
20. *The Economist* (July 12, 1941), p. 38.
21. Hancock and Gowing (eds.), pp. 337–338.

cision making was exceedingly important for the TUC and the trade union movement in general. Bevin had implemented the Citrine-Bevin concepts almost by fiat. And then by demonstrating their workability for five years, he provided the TUC with the chance to move permanently from its traditional defensive purpose as protector of the working class, to a practical and positive share in the responsibilities of economic management. This transformation was, however, fraught with danger, because it forced the movement to face the consequences of its own demands. But, at the same time, it gave the TUC the opportunity to exercise political and economic influence commensurate with the movement's numerical strength.

A NEW SOCIAL AND ECONOMIC CONTRACT

Significant public discussion about postwar reconstruction developed in early 1943. Before that time, the strain of war was so intense that the overriding question was not what kind of society there should be after the war, but, rather, whether Britain would exist at all. By December, 1942, however, there was growing confidence about the future.

German planes were still bombing English cities with devastating regularity. Yet the threat of invasion had diminished significantly as German attention became glued on an increasingly frustrating Russian front. The war was far from being won, but there seemed some basis for hope that the allies could win, even though ultimate victory might be several years off. Specifically, it was the successful British and American campaigns in North Africa during the fall of 1942 that launched public discussions about the postwar era in earnest.

The first thoughts about postwar Britain proceeded from memories of the only recently liquidated depression.[22]

---

22. In January, 1943, *The Times* (London), published a series of ten articles on postwar planning and full employment that stimulated a great deal of enthusiastic public discussion.

It was painfully realized that Britain had never really solved the problem of depression; only war production had done that. And some observers felt pessimistically that once repairs and restocking were completed and pent-up consumer demand was satisfied, depression conditions would very quickly reappear:

> Thus we should expect a second phase following the first—a period of relatively contracted demand, in which the number of would-be workers may well find themselves without a job—a delayed post-war depression linked with and partly caused by the high activity of immediate post-war days. . . . Let us once more look for guidance at what happened after the last war. . . .[23]

Discussions about how to deal with these problems drew heavily on the wartime experience. The war had been a difficult time for everyone, but full employment and government's comprehensive management of the economy on the basis of equality of sacrifice and fair shares, seemed to many a tonic in comparison to the interwar period when the nation's economic fabric failed so badly. Discussions about postwar Britain were therefore importantly concerned with drafting new economic and social principles that would permanently provide for a more prosperous, equitable, and secure society.

These concerns were only vaguely defined and infrequently discussed before the end of 1942, however, in spite of the official attention paid to the problems of postwar reconstruction and society before that time. Since the beginning of 1941, Arthur Greenwood and later Sir William Jowitt had served as Ministers Without Portfolio, charged with studying postwar problems. They had worked with the assistance of a small staff and a Committee of Ministers and with the Economic Committee of the Cabinet. Their job was to stimulate consideration of reconstruction problems within the regular departments, though not to produce detailed plans themselves. They also met frequently with representatives from both sides of industry to exchange ideas.

The *Report on Social Insurance* produced within the Ministry of Labour by Sir William Beveridge was, however,

---

23. Pigou, *The Transition from War to Peace*, p. 11.

the most influential work in galvanizing public interest in the question of reconstruction and postwar society.[24] Interestingly, the report took everyone by surprise, including Bevin, the Labour Minister. What was expected to be an inconspicuous technical report on social insurance, turned out to be a fundamental statement of human rights for a modern industrialized postwar Britain. Framed in strong and vigorous language, the report seemed to hit just the right chord when it was issued in December, 1942:

> Beveridge set out in detail a comprehensive scheme for social insurance for all citizens against sickness, poverty, and unemployment together with proposals for a national health service, family allowances, and the maintenance of full employment. No official report has ever aroused greater popular interest or enthusiasm.[25]

Nevertheless, the report angered Churchill and to some extent Bevin as well.[26] Both men, but especially Churchill, felt that a discussion of postwar reconstruction was premature and harmfully distracted attention from the war effort. Churchill also worried that the issues related to reconstruction might seriously divide the members of the Coalition and break down the general moratorium on partisan issues. He therefore initially ordered his ministers not to discuss the report publicly and even refused to see Beveridge. Three months later, in March, 1943, Churchill grudgingly acknowledged the enthusiastic public support for the "Beveridge Report" and, in a special broadcast, announced that the government would begin work on reconstruction planning. Slowly and fitfully over the next year and a half the government moved to involve itself in the process of defining and formulating a new economic and social "contract" for Britain.[27]

---

24. Bullock, II, 225.
25. Ibid.
26. Ibid., II, 226–227.
27. Professor Samuel Beer proposes the term "new social contract" in his book, *Modern British Politics*, p. 215. Bullock refers to this new "contract" in his book, II, 137. Both scholars agree that this new "contract" was first forged at the time that Bevin and Critrine worked out the principles maintaining voluntarism and establishing tripartite negotiations in May, 1940.

The publication of the White Paper, *Employment Policy*, in May, 1944, marked the climax of the debate on postwar reconstruction[28] and the consummation of the new economic and social contract. Hammered out by the members of the Coalition with the consultation of both sides of industry, the White Paper reflected the view that society should insure the availability of employment as an essential right, and that with that right came the opportunity for a "decent" standard of living in the broadest sense. The White Paper made it clear that postwar governments, whatever their political complexion, would "accept as one of their primary responsibilities the maintenance of a high and stable level of employment. . . ."[29]

This commitment to full employment was based on a fundamental acceptance of the Keynesian notion that employment levels are closely related to the health of the economy as a whole and that they are subject to control by government actions that raise or lower effective demand in the economy. The key instrument in the hands of government, according to the White Paper, is the government's influence over the level of total internal expenditures. However, the experience of full employment and government control over the economy in the five years of war had made it clear that full employment policy in peacetime would endow the huge trade union movement with powerful economic leverage. The conduct of economic policy would therefore depend, to an important extent, on whether government and labor could successfully extend their wartime collaboration.

The authors of the White Paper in 1944 recognized this point. They warned that "the success of the policy outlined in this Paper will ultimately depend on the understanding and support of the community as a whole—and especially on the efforts of employers and workers in industry. . . ."[30] In addition, they pinpointed the crucial issues between pro-

28. Ministry of Reconstruction, *Employment Policy*, Cmd. 6527 (May, 1944).
29. Ibid., p. 1.
30. Ibid.

ducers and government as the need for keeping wages and prices stable, and for maintaining the mobility of workers "between occupations and localities."[31] They added that workers would need to examine "their trade practices to ensure that they do not constitute a serious impediment to an expansionist economy and so defeat the object of a full employment programme."[32]

The White Paper was purposely vague about how the commitment to full employment should be translated into specific programs. This question was the subject of sharp partisan disagreement, and to have forced the issue in the negotiations that led to the White Paper might have jeopardized the chances for any agreement. Instead, the question of policy was deferred to the first postwar government, and therefore made one of the central issues in the 1945 election campaign. In this context, the Labour party as well as Sir William Beveridge and the TUC published their views about the postwar economy within a few months of the publication of the White Paper.[33]

The TUC was qualifiedly enthusiastic about the White Paper.[34] The General Council welcomed government commitment to full employment, although TUC leaders pointed out that they had urged successive governments since 1930 to adopt Keynes's proposals for ending unemployment. Full employment would, of course, be a personal boon for every workingman and for the labor movement in general. However, they also made it clear that full employment by itself was not enough. They could not accept "as adequate a policy which merely aimed at stabilizing employment by evening out the major fluctuations in trade."[35]

The TUC defined its goals more specifically in its *Interim Report on Post-War Reconstruction,* published

31. Ibid., p. 16.
32. Ibid., p. 19.
33. Labour Party, *Full Employment and Financial Policy;* Beveridge, *Full Employment in a Free Society;* and Trades Union Congress, *Interim Report on Post-War Reconstruction.*
34. Citrine, "The Month," *Labour,* p. 290.
35. Trades Union Congress, *Interim Report on Post-War Reconstruction,* p. 3.

shortly after the White Paper in June, 1944. The TUC report declared that the trade union movement was determined to gain a "decisive share in the actual control of the economic life of the nation,"[36] but at the same time must be free to continue to function without state interference and otherwise be left to represent its members as it saw fit—especially in determining wages, hours, and the conditions of work. In return and mindful of its enhanced power, the TUC pledged that the trade union movement would continue to act reasonably and responsibly in the spirit of the wartime collaboration, in order to permit full employment to benefit all parts of the society.

The TUC's specific proposals contained in the *Interim Report* called for changes in the economic system that were not new. They were almost identical to those first presented in the 1932 report, modified somewhat to accommodate the wartime experience. They differed from the White Paper primarily in their explicit call for the gradual development of state control over at least the key sectors of production. Among the most important proposals were:

1. The establishment of a National Industrial Council to advise the government on all aspects of industrial policy. The council would have trade union and employer representatives and its own staff.

2. State control over banking, foreign trade, credit, and land utilization. In addition, the state would nationalize the fuel and power, transport, and iron and steel and cotton industries and put them under the control of public boards.

3. In those industries not nationalized, government would exercise powerful indirect control through its enormous purchasing and licensing powers. Price controls would also be used vigorously.

TUC leaders felt that the implementation of these proposals in the context of full employment would go a long way toward achieving their major goals of gaining a permanent share in the control of economic life, while retaining

36. Walker, "TUC and Post-War Reconstruction," *Labour and Trade Bulletin,* p. 6.

voluntarism in industrial relations. The establishment of a National Industrial Council, for example, would provide the TUC with important access and influence on broad economic decision making, and nationalization would, they felt, involve trade unionists in production decisions at every level down to the shop floor.

Correspondingly, the TUC's strategy to implement these proposals depended, as it had for the previous decade, on a victory for the Labour party at the next general election. Trade unionism's relationship with the Conservatives had considerably improved during the war because of the immense respect for Churchill. But the TUC and the labor movement still had a complex set of ideological and personal ties to the Labour party, and from a practical point of view the TUC had made a significant investment in collaborating with Labour on the development of common economic policy plans. Trades Union Congress leaders, in 1945, were anxious to cash in on that investment.

CONCLUSION

The TUC in 1945 was no longer a "voice in the wilderness." Rather, it stood at the very center of economic decision making as a full negotiating partner with business and government. The goals that Walter Citrine and Ernest Bevin framed for the TUC following the General Strike were largely realized: the TUC became the center of trade unionism before the Second World War and then, because of the war, the TUC began to consult fully and regularly with government about every issue that directly or indirectly concerned the interests of trade unionists. Further, a consensus about a new set of economic purposes for postwar Britain, with its pledge of continuing full employment, promised that the TUC would continue to exercise important influence on public policy.

These achievements, however, posed new problems. The war had provided a compelling rationale for trade

unionism to collaborate. Individual unions almost unques-
tioningly accepted the TUC's leadership on all national
issues, and in turn, the General Council fully cooperated
with government to spur the war effort. The war thus endowed the TUC with important new power as well as restraints on the unfettered use of that power. When the
war ended, most of these restraints were quickly dismantled,
but government, nevertheless, continued to need trade union
cooperation for its policies that sought to deal with recurring
economic crises and to fulfill the terms of the new economic
and social contract. However, it was difficult to gain cooperation in a voluntary context. "Collaboration or conflict"
thus became the central question facing the TUC during the
postwar years. How the TUC answered this question was
centrally important to the course of economic policy after
1945.

-→≫⟦ 4 ⟧≪←-

Labour Government
and Producer Group Politics:
The Wages Bargain of 1948

T HE Labour party won the 1945 election and, for the
first time, formed a majority government which took office
committed to fulfill the terms of the new social and economic
contract. Its pledge of far-reaching economic changes pointed
to the continuation of government's management of the
economy and an expanding scope of public policy. This,
Samuel Beer suggests, dictated that producing groups in the
society be given greater power, since "insofar as government
has committed itself to intervention in the economy, it must
have access to or control over instrumentalities that are in
command of producers."[1] In turn, the realities of getting
elected and of governing in the postwar years produced a
convergence of party programs, despite their continuing differences over the premises of action, i.e., their opposing con-
ceptions of "class and community."[2] Governments of both
parties thus sought the "advice, acquiescence, or approval"
of producer groups for their economic policies through a system of consultations that often became full-scale negotiations.[3] The operational requirement for successful producer
group politics is that government and producer groups be
willing and able to use the negotiating process to reach an
agreement on the shape of policy and then that both sides
proceed to fulfill their part of the bargain effectively.
 The history of the TUC provides an example that illus-

1. *Modern British Politics,* p. 321.
2. Ibid., p. 403.
3. Ibid., chap. XII.

trates the origins of producer group power. Increments in Trades Union Congress power vis-à-vis the government occurred largely in response to the expansion of government control over economic affairs, especially during the First World War and more dramatically during the Second. Yet, although the TUC became an important partner in economic decision making during the war, the pressures for collaboration in the war effort strongly restrained vigorous bargaining.

Beer cites the wages bargain of 1948 between the TUC and the Attlee government as the first example of the functioning of the new producer group politics. After examining the events most immediately related to the bargain, he concludes that its development was a concise exercise in purposive negotiations that throws light on "the power structure of postwar Britain, illustrating the vast power of organized producer groups . . . [and demonstrates the] extension of government power over the behavior of those engaged in production," from which organized groups gain a strong bargaining position.[4]

The examination of the same wages bargain, however, from the broader perspective of a sixteen-month process that developed in four phases, offers a different view. While confirming that management of the economy compels government to seek the cooperation of producer groups by means of extensive consultations and negotiations, the negotiations in 1946–1948 were lacking in direction and focus. Neither side stated clearly what it would or would not do, and the government and the TUC acted hesitantly and timidly toward each other. The final agreement in March, 1948, was as much a surrender by the TUC as a bargain. Yet the wages bargain of 1948 is the only example in the postwar era when the TUC not only reached agreement with government on incomes policy, but also kept its part of the agreement by holding a wages freeze for more than two years.

These findings require amending Beer's comments on producer group politics, especially as they relate to the be-

4. Ibid., pp. 208–209.

havior of the TUC. The unevenness of the negotiations and then the conclusion of the bargain were both attributable to the force of the traditional relationship between trade unionism and the Labour Party. Ideological, organizational, and personal ties acted to inhibit the negotiations at some points and to spur them toward agreement at others. Comprehensive bargaining, on the other hand, failed to resolve the substantive disagreements between the TUC and the government. The notion of wage restraint in a setting of full employment fundamentally clashed with the purposes of the trade union movement, and the prospect for agreement on a wages freeze was unpalatable to many on the General Council regardless of considerations of the national interest. Further, the TUC's lack of authority made those same leaders wonder whether, if they agreed to wage restraint, the agreement would then be subject to veto by their members.[5] Later, however, as economic crisis prodded the government to demand more urgently cooperation from the TUC, the force of traditional loyalties between the political and industrial wings of the labor movement conspired to convince the General Council to decide in favor of collaboration instead of conflict.

DECLINE INTO CRISIS

The TUC held a unique and enviable position in its relations with the new Labour government. It had helped not only to define the programs and set the ground rules for its own role in the management of the economy, but a number of its own leaders were serving in the new government. Also, Beer points out that the Attlee government kept its programmatic promises with a systematic and unique fidelity that quickly paid off the TUC's long investment in the Labour party with dividends. By the end of 1946, the TUC had achieved its primary goals: through the program of national-

5. See chap. 2.

ization and the development of thorough consultations the TUC was exercising a "decisive share in the actual control of the economic life of the nation,"[6] and with the removal of many wartime restrictions and the repeal of the Trade Disputes Act the TUC was able, with minor restrictions, to represent its constituent members as it saw fit. Therefore, as economic difficulties began to proliferate in late 1946, the TUC held a powerful and self-satisfying position.

The symptoms of Britain's underlying economic problems were difficult to perceive during 1945 and the first half of 1946. American and Canadian loans helped to mask Britain's financial weakness by underwriting the standard of living. Shortages of housing, food, and virtually all consumer goods were still acute, but these shortages were no worse than Britain had endured during five years of war.

By the latter half of 1946, however, more visible signs of impending trouble were surfacing. Trade deficits were increasing each month and it was becoming clearer that the foreign loan money, programmed to support the economy until 1950, would be exhausted much earlier unless drastic import restrictions were quickly imposed.[7] Current shortages and imbalances developed even more seriously as British industry began to recover and make larger demands for material resources. (The earliest signs of these problems occurred in the coal industry which suffered from manpower shortages and seriously worn-out and obsolete equipment.) Finally, the rate of inflation was increasing rapidly, caused both by material shortages and by a deluge of large wage increases.

Many in the Cabinet viewed these mounting economic problems from the perspective of their personal wartime experience in the Coalition government when they had administered programs based on rigorous physical controls.[8] They felt the government should seek to create a balance between

6. Walker, "TUC and Post-War Reconstruction," *Labour and Trade Bulletin*, p. 6.
7. Central Office of Information, *Britain's Economic Position*, p. 1.
8. Hancock and Gowing (eds.), *British War Economy*, p. 337.

manpower and material resources, a balance expressed in numerical terms.

This emphasis on a manpower budget, in turn, placed added importance on the development of trade union-government cooperation on the issues of labor direction and wages. Government needed trade union help in providing manpower for those industries whose full production the government considered most critical to the economy. Selective wage incentives and especially wage controls would help to restrain inflation and the cost of export products.

In full confidence the Cabinet initially expected to have the TUC's support for whatever policies it decided were necessary to meet the growing difficulties. After all, the government was developing and implementing a program of economic reforms that to a significant extent was shaped and ratified by the whole labor movement. Also, the government had been careful to fulfill its promises with the full participation of trade unionists at every level. On the other hand, for TUC leaders, labor direction and wage controls were unpleasant possibilities to contemplate because they assailed the fundamental purpose of the union movement. In sum, as the government began to formulate its strategy for dealing with growing economic problems in 1946, it, as well as the unions, began to face the first example of the contradictions in their alliance.

NEGOTIATIONS

October, 1946–January, 1947. Months before the coal crisis of February, 1947, shattered the guarded optimism of the first twenty months of the postwar era, the government began quietly to deal with the first symptoms of fuel shortages and wage inflation. The Minister of Labour, George Isaacs, raised the problem of manpower distribution, wage inflation, and supply-demand problems with business and labor for the first time at a meeting of the National Joint Advisory Coun-

cil on October 30, 1946. Further discussions ensued at
government initiative and continued through December.
Government and TUC representatives approached each
other warily. The government was quite reluctant to stage a
frontal assault on sacred union prerogatives and therefore
made no specific demands for union cooperation. TUC
representatives, on the other hand, tried to avoid substantive
discussions while publicly appearing to be concerned and
conciliatory so as not to embarrass and damage the government's credibility. In total, these discussions produced nothing and the resulting White Paper, *Statement on the Economic Conditions Affecting Relations Between Employers
and Workers* (Cmd. 7018), was notable only for how little it
said. It reviewed the economic situation in the most general
terms, but failed to reach any conclusions except that everyone needed to make a greater effort. The General Council, in
its own report on the meetings, revealed that the talks had
failed because the unions had made it clear they would not
consider any restrictions on their rights to free collective
bargaining:

> It was made clear to the Minister and the Government that
> the approval of the General Council to the first White Paper was
> on the definite understanding that Unions would continue to be
> free to submit wages applications as formerly where this was
> found to be necessary. Nothing in the White Paper was to be
> taken as restricting the rights of Unions to make claims through
> normal collective bargaining arrangements. Such claims should
> be considered on their merits.[9]

The Attlee government's first attempt to gain TUC
cooperation therefore proved fruitless. The TUC foreclosed
meaningful discussion by ruling out the possibility that it
would agree to any form of incomes policy. Yet, the government itself insured that the discussions would be unproductive by failing to ask the TUC explicitly for anything. Minister of Labour Isaacs (a former member of the General Coun-

---

9. Trades Union Congress, *Report of Proceedings, Annual Trades Union
Congress* (1947), p. 219.

cil), went no further than staging a sparring match that never got to the point. The government's only strategy was to present the facts of the situation to both sides of industry and hope that business and the trade unions would draw the right conclusions and subsequently decide to offer cooperation. This did not happen, and the talks ended in confusion, without progress.

February, 1947–June, 1947. The next phase in what eventually developed into the wages bargain of 1948, opened on February 7, 1947, with the announcement by Emanuel Shinwell, Minister for Fuel and Power, to the House of Commons, that coal supplies had grown so short due to the extremely cold weather that electricity service for commercial users in a large part of the country would have to be suspended immediately. This announcement came as a profound shock to almost everyone. It added the element of tangible crisis to the equation that had led nowhere in the earlier discussions between the TUC and the government.

The government responded to the fuel crisis in February by announcing it would take firmer control over the economy, especially over the allocation of material resources. Eleven days after Shinwell's announcement, the government published the *Economic Survey for 1947,* which stressed physical economic planning and for the first time established explicit priorities and production targets for the year, industry by industry.[10] Then, on March 10, Sir Stafford Cripps told the House of Commons that the government intended to establish an interdepartmental economic planning staff, to be headed by a Chief Planning Officer and advised by an Economic Planning Board having representatives of both sides of industry. The purpose of the planning staff would be to plan for the long term, but it would be concerned also with reviewing current problems in order ". . . to weigh up the calls on productive resources and to recommend how re-

10. Treasury, Cmd. 7046 (February, 1947).

sources and requirements can best be brought into balance continually."[11]

In practice, however, the government continued to act sluggishly and timidly. Sir Edward Plowdon was appointed as the first Chief Planning Officer about two weeks after Cripps's speech. It was not until May, however, that the Planning Staff was organized and then another two months until the government appointed the Economic Planning Board. Throughout, the government continued to avoid asking the TUC for help,[12] despite the General Council's professed nervousness about the intense, though brief, surge in unemployment levels to almost 2 million men that occurred in the wake of the fuel crisis.[13]

July, 1947–March, 1948. The third phase in the unfolding crisis began at the end of July, 1947. Under the terms of the postwar loans, Britain declared sterling to be freely convertible on July 5, 1947. Within a few weeks, however, stories appeared in the press that Britain's international payments position was deteriorating rapidly. The General Council, now seriously alarmed, pressed the government for details.[14]

Herbert Morrison, the Lord President of the Council, told TUC leaders in an emergency meeting on August 2 that the press reports were substantially correct. Although the country was making excellent progress domestically, he said, its external situation was becoming critical and the two loans that had been "sought in order to enable us to keep going until 1950 without having to make extensive cuts in imports, were rapidly becoming exhausted."[15] He added:

---

11. House of Commons. *Parliamentary Debates,* vol. 434 (March 10, 1947), cols. 970–971.
12. Cripps put the government's timidity toward the trade union movement quite explicitly in his statement on the White Paper: "In fact, the White Paper contains a wages policy, but not the sort of policy that some people are demanding. We are proceeding upon the basis that despite the difficulties created by full employment, employers and employees should remain free to settle the conditions of work or wages in industry where the employers are private or public companies or corporations." Ibid., col. 193.
13. Trades Union Congress (1947), p. 220.
14. Ibid., p. 567.
15. Ibid., p. 568.

The Cabinet thought it only right and proper that the General Council of the T.U.C. should be advised of those proposals which the Government had in mind to make to Parliament which would directly affect work-people and their Trade Unions. The Employers' organisations would be similarly consulted.[16]

The proposals that Morrison outlined at that meeting surprised the General Council members because the government so suddenly was challenging the TUC on heretofore untouchable issues. The government proposed:

1. Labor Direction: The reinstatement of the wartime Control of Engagements Order. This would allow the Minister of Labour to divert manpower to essential industries producing strategically important export and domestic items.

2. Hours of Work: The government asked the General Council to make representations to their member unions in order to get agreements on lengthening working days.

3. Wage Movements: The government said it wanted to know more about wage movements in order to be able to anticipate "more accurately and extensively than hitherto on the movements of wages and their possible economic consequences."[17] Therefore, the government proposed to establish in the Ministry of Labour a branch to collect and collate information on wages and hours.

Wages control by legislation or by other means of compulsion was not mentioned. To some TUC leaders this absence of an initiative on wages in so critical a situation, other than the curious proposal to collect information on wage movements, was a hint that the government was still hesitant to act against its trade union allies and instead was seeking a compromise.[18] Perhaps, they reasoned, the government was willing to extend a guarantee to the TUC that there would be no wage controls if the General Council would agree to at least a measure of labor direction and longer hours of work.[19]

The Prime Minister delivered to the House of Commons on August 6 his public statement on the payments

---

16. Ibid.
17. Ibid., pp. 568–569.
18. Vincent Tewson, former General Secretary of the TUC, 1946–1960, now retired. Interview, August 11, 1969.
19. Allen, *Trade Unions and the Government*, pp. 283–284.

crisis together with the proposals that Morrison had outlined earlier and a thinly veiled call for voluntary wage restraint. The TUC responded with a series of statements of solid support and promises of help. That afternoon the General Council met in special session and quickly agreed to the reinstatement of the Control of Engagements Order and promised to consult with its constituent unions to see whether it would be possible to extend hours of work. At the same time, TUC representatives on the National Joint Advisory Council strongly supported a statement expressing the full approval of both the unions and employers for the government's actions in the crisis. Three weeks later at Congress, the General Council concluded its report on the economic situation with a further and unusually strong endorsement of the government's efforts to deal with the economic problems:

> The General Council have already assured the Government of the determination of the Trade Union Movement to do all in their power to assist the country in this time of crisis. Immediately upon the close of Congress contact will be made with the Government to get the clearest possible picture of the situation and to sit down with the appropriate Ministers to consider the plans of the Government for meeting the immediate position. The Trade Union Movement, like the nation of which it is part, has never failed to rise to an emergency. The emergency is here.[20]

The General Council hoped that its rapid and positive response to the Attlee speech of August 6 would be taken by the government as the consummation of an understanding that included assurances that voluntary wages bargaining would remain sacrosanct. Vincent Tewson, addressing Congress on September 2, made it clear that the TUC expected the government to go no further, although he indicated he was far from sure about this:

> One further point: you see in the Supplementary Report a brief reference to wage movements, and you find there that a statement is made that the Government's attitude in regard to this matter is that they have rejected the doctrine that wages

20. Trades Union Congress (1947), p. 574.

should be settled by the Government. They have decided to set up a department for the collection of information. We know that there is no objection to this department, but I want to issue a word of warning. At the moment we have a sympathetic Minister of Labour, and it should not be regarded that the agreement to the setting up of this department in any way involves a recognition that this is to be the thin edge of the wedge in the dislodging of the attitude of the Cabinet on this matter to which reference has been made. But first you have supply of information, then the word "guidance" is brought in and down the slippery slope you may go until you get from "information" and "guidance" to "instruction."[21]

The members of the General Council not only put their faith in the existence of an understanding on wages, but they generally were highly sympathetic to the government's situation. Virtually all council members, but especially Deakin, Williamson, Geddes, and Tewson, were concerned that the government's failure to deal successfully with the economic crisis would jeopardize the labor movement's own position.[22] They were at once fearful that the failure of the Labour government to solve the crisis might precipitate a new depression and mass unemployment, and mindful too that the Labour government had kept its pledge to maintain full employment. There was, in their view, no feasible alternative to continued support for the Attlee government.[23]

September, 1947–March, 1948. The fourth phase of the developing bargain opened shortly after the 1947 Congress adjourned. September was a key month for the submission of annual wages claims to collective bargaining, and the usual round of negotiations got underway in the second week of the month. In the midst of these negotiations Minister of Labour Isaacs sent letters to both sides reminding them of the Prime Minister's statement to Parliament in

21. Ibid., p. 366.
22. Tewson interview, see *n.* 18; Allen, *Trade Union Leadership,* p. 130.
23. Ibid.

August exhorting workers to avoid pressing for wage increases
not tied to increases in productivity, especially for increases
designed to maintain wage differentials.[24] The General
Council reacted swiftly and angrily. They considered the
Isaacs letter an insult to the union movement's good faith
in supporting the government's economic policies; a breach
of the implied bargain; and an intemperate encroachment on
the collective bargaining process.[25] They pressed the Prime
Minister for an apology and assurances that the government
would keep out of wages negotiations in the future. Attlee,
in a meeting with the General Council on October 1, quickly
extended these assurances and his apologies, but he also used
the meeting to move a step further with the TUC. He asked
the TUC leaders to meet with the Minister of Labour and
the Minister of Economic Affairs, as well as with the Chancellor to discuss the general problems of wage stability. The
General Council accepted reluctantly and two meetings followed on October 7 and October 29.

Hugh Dalton on October 7 and Sir Stafford Cripps on
October 29 told the General Council that the wages issue
could no longer simply be ignored.[26] After reviewing the
economic situation in detail, Cripps, Minister for Economic
Affairs and later Chancellor after Dalton was forced to re-
sign, emphasized to the council the government's view that
the solution to the payments crisis depended most on increasing British exports.[27] However, the success of the efforts
to increase exports depended, Cripps said, on getting manpower into the important export industries and producing
goods at costs that would keep British prices competitively
attractive. He pointed out that after the First World War,
government had wrongly and without success sacrificed the

---

24. Trades Union Congress, *Report of Proceedings, Annual Trades Union
Congress* (1948), pp. 288–289.
25. Ibid.
26. By this time Sir Stafford Cripps had given up his former position as
president of the Board of Trade in order to take charge of the government's
stepped-up efforts to plan the economy. He was appointed to the newly
created post of Minister for Economic Affairs, which supplanted in importance the post of Chief Planning Officer.
27. Trades Union Congress (1948), p. 289.

standard of living and permitted high rates of unemployment in order to create and maintain lower price levels. In contrast, the Labour government was pledged to defend full employment and therefore had to rely on the responsible actions of the trade unions in restraining wage inflation.

The members of the General Council accepted the validity of Cripps's argument. Its thrust clashed sharply, however, with their responsibilities as trade union leaders pledged to protect the interests of their men—which meant continuously pressing for wage increases and better working conditions. A majority on the council, however, led by Deakin from inside the movement and encouraged by Bevin from outside, were coming to believe in 1947 that the national interest was wholly bound up with their responsibility to their unions.[28] For this group, including Vincent Tewson, the TUC General Secretary, the argument that wage increases without previous increases in productivity were counterproductive, was sensible. Only Deakin, though, among the union leaders was, at that time, willing to take this stand publicly.

To prod the General Council, both Cripps and Dalton raised the possibility that the cost-of-living subsidies might have to be ended.[29] Vincent Tewson commented in an interview that the subsidies issue was, to the trade union movement at that time, one of the thorniest and yet most important. Food subsidies were especially important because they allowed the workingman to mitigate the problems of inordinately high food prices caused by severe import restrictions. Food subsidies did not alleviate food shortages, but they did make it possible for even the lowest paid worker to afford a reasonable share of what there was to buy. In short, the subsidies were supplemental income. The problem by the end of 1947 was that food and other subsidies were a growing burden on an already strained budget. The government very much wanted to find a way to end them, but for a Labour government this was politically and socially a difficult mat-

28. Allen, *Trade Unions and the Government*, pp. 288–289.
29. Trades Union Congress (1948), loc. cit.

64 CHAPTER 4

ter. However, in the context of these negotiations Dalton
and Cripps used the issue as leverage against the council.
Intimidated on the subsidies issue, the General Council
agreed to review its position on wages again, as part of an
overall examination of the interrelated problems of the cost-
of-living subsidies, profits, price controls, and wages. Six
weeks later the council published its tentative findings in an
Interim Report on the Economic Situation.
The report urged the continuation of the subsidies program despite unreasonably mounting costs. It did recognize
that the government could not make an open-ended promise
to continue subsidies regardless of their effect on the movements of wages and profits over which the government did
not exercise control. Yet, it fell far short of issuing a clear-cut
call for its constituent unions to protect the future of subsidies by dampening their wage claims.[30] Rather, the General Council emphasized, above all else, that trade unions
must continue to guard jealously their rights to voluntary
collective bargaining:

> This policy, by which Government controls and subsidises
> prices and trade unions remain independent of Government
> control, free from specific restrictions on their right to pursue
> wage claims and yet willing to play their part in the maintenance
> of price stability, has proved remarkably successful in every way.
> . . . The present and immediate future is not a time during
> which Great Britain would be well advised to abandon or to
> modify substantially any aspect of price stability which we have
> pursued ever since 1940.[31]

The report thus did not reject the government's position outright, but instead largely evaded the issue. The majority of the council, by this time, had swung over to Deakin's
view that although wage restraints were bitter medicine, the
control of inflation and the development of economic stability would provide more lasting gains than short-term pay

---

30. It is interesting to note that the 1948 Congress Report interpreted the
Interim Report as a TUC call for vigorous wage restraint, although it was
not. The report was, of course, written after the council had finally agreed
to wage restraints in March, 1948.
31. Trades Union Congress, *Interim Report on the Economic Situation*, p. 5.

increases.[32] However, only a minority of the General Council members, even under the most intense prodding, were yet ready to rewrite General Council policy on so sensitive an issue. At that time, therefore, the sum of their responses was that the General Council was not prepared to go any further than the terms of its earlier bargain on labor direction and hours.

The report thus still left the negotiations at an impasse. Then, without public warning, the government on February 4, 1948, broke the impasse unilaterally by issuing a White Paper, *Statement on Personal Incomes, Costs, and Prices,* that declared there was no justification for any further wage increases without commensurate increases in productivity.[33]

The General Council reacted angrily. It complained it had not been consulted, as had been the custom since almost the beginning of the Second World War. Substantively, it protested that the White Paper put the blame for Britain's economic problems and the burden of their solution almost entirely on the issue of wage inflation, while only superficially touching on the effects of profits and dividends. It also criticized the paper's vague treatment of the relationship between productivity and wages. How would unions know what productivity increases justified new wage claims? And, finally, what was to be the fate of claims that had already been entered?[34]

Yet, despite this angry reaction, the General Council immediately agreed to the government's call for a new series of negotiations. Stung by the White Paper, or perhaps relieved that it made collaboration appear more respectable, the General Council suddenly became eager to work out a compromise and the ensuing discussion quickly produced an agreement. First, a special committee of TUC leaders led by Arthur Deakin, Lincoln Evans, Will Lawther, Tom Wil-

---

32. Lord Geddes, retired former member of the General Council and General Secretary of the Post Office Workers, and Lord Williamson, retired former member of the General Council and General Secretary of the National Union of General and Municipal Workers. Joint interview, July 2, 1969.
33. Cmd. 7321.
34. Trades Union Congress (1948), pp. 289–290.

liamson, and Vincent Tewson met with Clement Attlee, Sir
Stafford Cripps, Ernest Bevin (Foreign Secretary), Herbert
Morrison, and George Isaacs on February 11. The General
Council wasted no time at that meeting in spelling out the
conditions under which it felt it could cooperate on wage
restraint:

    1. Subsidies should be continued.

    2. Price controls should be vigorously enforced.

    3. Profits and dividends should be restrained.

    4. Wages that are "substandard" should not be re-
strained.

    5. Wage increases should be permitted, based on in-
creases in productivity.

    6. Wage differentials should be safeguarded.

    7. The system of collective bargaining should be un-
impaired.[35]

Sir Stafford Cripps responded indirectly to the TUC in
a speech to the House of Commons on the following day in
which he announced government actions that, in part, met
TUC terms for agreement:

    1. Prices subject to the price control system would be
frozen at their level of January 31, 1948.

    2. Margins of profit for distribution would be fixed at
a rate no higher than at present.

    3. No wage increases would be allowed to raise the
prices of goods covered by cost-plus controls.

    4. The Federation of British Industries and other simi-
lar organizations would submit to the Chancellor of the
Exchequer within a month a plan for reducing prices and
profits.[36]

Six days later, on February 18, the General Council met
to consider the recommendation of its special committee that
the terms of the White Paper be accepted on condition that
the government continue to press for the implementation of

35. Trades Union Congress, *Report of Proceedings at a Special Conference of
Executive Committees of Affiliated Organizations, March 24, 1948*, p. 10.
36. House of Commons. *Parliamentary Debates*, vol. 447 (February 12, 1948),
cols. 592–602.

the points Cripps accepted in his speech on February 11, although they did not meet TUC demands completely.[37] They further recommended that a Special Conference of Trade Union Executives meet in a month to ratify the agreement, and that the agreement be reviewed every three months thereafter. The General Council approved these recommendations that day and the bargain was sealed.

A Special Conference of Trade Union Executives met in London on March 24. During the intervening month the government successfully convinced the employers' associations to support limitations on profits and dividends. This was important in the discussions at the special conference. The vote approving the General Council's actions was approximately 5 million to 2 million. It was a victory for the General Council, attributable to the sheer force of the personalities at the trade union center, but it also carried a warning. The 2 million votes cast in opposition to the bargain foretold serious trouble for the wages freeze if the government did not live up to its part of the bargain or if the cost of living continued to rise so rapidly. The opposition did not quarrel with the leadership's analysis of the crisis. Rather, it objected to the General Council's agreement to allow the workingman to carry the burden of a freeze, while restraints of prices and profits were of secondary importance. Additionally, many delegates to the conference were disillusioned with the Labour government, which they felt had sacrificed their interests instead of first moving against private business.[38]

IMPLEMENTATION OF THE WAGES BARGAIN: 1948–1951

The major elements of the 1948 bargain were the TUC's acceptance of a freeze on almost all wage increases; the government's promise to enforce strong price controls; and the

---

37. Trades Union Congress (1948), p. 290.
38. Trades Union Congress, *Report of Proceedings at a Special Conference* . . . *March 24, 1948*, p. 22.

employers organizations' agreement to limit severely dividends and profits. This bargain worked to slow inflation markedly after March, and continued to be effective until military rearmament in 1950–1951 produced renewed price inflation. However, the success of the bargain did not solve Britain's fundamental economic problems and the Labour government in September, 1949, devalued the pound and thereby acknowledged the failure of its efforts to stabilize the economy by direct price and wage controls.

TABLE 4.1.   WAGES AND PRICES, 1947–1950

Year Month	Wages June 30, 1947 = 100	Retail Prices June 17, 1947 = 100	Retail Prices June 17, 1947 = 100
	(All workers)	(All items)	(Food)
1947			
June	100	100	100
October	102	101	100.6
1948			
March	105	106	108.8
June	106	110	113.5
October	107	108	107.6
1949			
March	108	109	108.0
June	109	111	115.5
October	109	112	119
1950			
March	110	113	121.3

Source: Central Statistical Office. *Monthly Digest of Statistics*. June, 1950, table 149, p. 121.

TABLE 4.2.   VALUE AND VOLUME OF EXTERNAL TRADE[a], 1946–1949

Year	Retained Imports (1938 = 100)	Value of Imports (1 £ millions)	Exports[b] (1938 = 100)	Value of Exports (1 £ millions)
1946	68	108.4	99	76.2
1947	78	149.5	109	94.9
1948	81	173.2	136	131.8
1949	87	189.4	151	148.7

Source: Central Statistical Office. *Monthly Digest of Statistics*. June, 1950, table 110, p. 88.
[a] Quantities revalued at 1938 prices and expressed as a percentage of the average in 1938.
[b] Including relief and rehabilitation supplies to liberated countries.

TABLE 4.3. GOLD AND DOLLAR RESERVES, 1947–1950

Year, Month	(US $, millions)
1947	
June 30	2,410
September 30	2,383
1948	
March 31	2,241
June 30	1,920
September 30	1,777
1949	
March 31	1,912
June 30	1,651
September 30	1,425
1950	
March 31	1,984

Source: Central Statistical Office. *Monthly Digest of Statistics.* June, 1950, table 147, p. 120.

Tables 4.1, 4.2, and 4.3 document the successes of wages freeze and price restraint, and present a profile of the British economy through this period:

1. *Wages:* Wages had moved up 5 points in the nine months from June, 1947, until the ratification of the bargain in March, 1948. After that, wages increased by only 4 points in the eighteen-month period from March, 1948, until devaluation in September, 1949.

2. *Prices:* For the same period, from June, 1947, until March, 1948, the prices of all retail items had moved up 6 points. But in the following eighteen months, while wage restraint was in effect, overall prices increased 6 points while food prices went up 10, even though wages were rising only 4 points.

3. *Trade and Financial Position:* Exports increased faster than imports during the period of wage restraint, as the government had hoped. The rate of increase, however, was not enough to erase the deficit, which remained at a constant, absolute level of about £40 million in 1949. This deficit had a depressive effect on gold and dollar reserves which fell from about £2.240 billion in 1947 to £1.425 billion in 1949 at the time of devaluation.

CONCLUSION

The wages bargain of 1948 was a positive accomplishment in that an agreement was reached. However more valuable it might have been if attained months earlier, the TUC's effective implementation of that agreement, even though only partially successful, did contribute to the government's efforts to stabilize the economy.

The negotiations leading to the agreement demonstrated the relationship of increased producer group power to government's efforts to manage the economy. Full employment especially provided the TUC with important bargaining leverage because government, striving to fulfill the terms of the new social and economic contract and also to treat the economic crisis, had to ask the TUC urgently for help in restraining wages. However, the negotiations for wage restraint were not a concise exercise in purposive bargaining, as Beer suggested. Rather, they lacked direction and purpose, suffering from the inhibitions that the government and the TUC displayed toward each other. There was agreement for wage restraint for the same reason that the negotiations dragged on for sixteen months—because the force of traditional relations between the Labour party and the TUC acted at some points to retard and at other points to spur agreement. The terms of the bargain in February, 1948, were less important to its conclusion than was the influence of these traditional relations.

For the government's part, Attlee and his colleagues showed great deference toward the TUC. They were enormously reluctant to take actions they thought would infringe on trade union prerogatives. The Cabinet held this stance even when it faced economic problems the solutions of which depended on gaining the TUC's cooperation for policies that would compromise its interests. In December, 1946, and again in November, 1947, the Cabinet swallowed hard but accepted the TUC's refusals to change its position on wages. Even in February, 1947, when faced with a difficult fuel crisis, the government failed to ask the TUC for direct and specific help in manning the mines.

Organizational and financial relations between the TUC and the Labour party account for some of the government's inhibition. But Martin Harrison, in his study of trade unions and the Labour party, offers what is probably the most incisive answer. Harrison concludes that "The Labour Party is bound to the unions not just by cash and card votes, but by personalities and doctrines, common experience and sentiment—and mutual advantage.[39] Thus there continued to be the strong influence of class consciousness and a fundamental agreement on the power and purpose of government. In this way, TUC leaders exercised significant but largely negative influence by inhibiting government policy as it affected trade union interests.[40]

At other points in the long series of negotiations, notably when the government faced its most serious economic problems, the force of Harrison's argument worked in the opposite direction. Contrary to Beer's suggestion that producer groups hold a *stronger* bargaining position in government attempts to manage and plan the economy, the TUC felt it was in an almost *helpless* position when government most urgently demanded cooperation. For example, in August, 1947, and again in March, 1948, both of which were moments of extreme crisis, the TUC surrendered to government pressure for agreement with very little resistance.

Again, the special ties between the TUC and the Labour party came into play.[41] There was displayed a strong feeling of identity by the General Council members with the Labour government. It was "their" government. It had delivered on its promises of economic and social reform.[42] It had kept

---

39. *Trade Unions and the Labour Party Since 1945*, p. 340.
40. For example, Allen cites Bevin's influence on Attlee in convincing him not to regulate wages. See Allen, *Trade Unions and the Government*, p. 283.
41. Allen in *Trade Unions and the Government* points out that Arthur Deakin's personal loyalty to the Labour government in part prompted him to change his previous views on the wages issue. This kind of loyalty was expressed in a personal interview this observer had with Lord Geddes and Lord Williamson, both important leaders of the General Council during this period. (July 2, 1969.)
42. This point was strongly emphasized by Florence Hancock, Chairman of the TUC, in her opening remarks in support of wage restraint to the Special Conference of Trade Union Executives on March 24, 1948. See Trades Union Congress, *Report of Special Conference of March 24, 1948*, p. 7.

its pledge to maintain full employment, even against some very powerful arguments in favor of deflation in 1947. And moreover, the ties of personalities, doctrines, common experience, and sentiment bound the TUC's loyalty to the Labour government.

TUC leaders were also concerned that agreement at critical points was the price the TUC had to pay to continue to be at the "table." All parties had made a commitment in the 1944 White Paper to continue full employment in the postwar years, but only a Labour government had held office up to that time. Memories of the depression and Tory "indifference" to unemployment were still fresh. The Tory commitment to full employment was therefore still suspect by union leaders and the incumbency of a Labour government was considered "essential."[43] Finally, TUC leaders feared that if they did not agree at those critical moments, or simply left the "table" to sulk, that the Labour government would reluctantly legislate its industrial policies in order to keep its programmatic commitment to manage the economy aggressively.

Producer group politics in the wages bargain of 1948 thus "worked" in the sense that an agreement was concluded and was effectively implemented. Comprehensive bargaining failed, however, to resolve the substantive objections that the TUC had to wage restraint. Rather, producer group politics "worked" because the traditional alliance and loyalties between the TUC and the Labour party, coupled with the magnitude of the crisis, overcame the General Council's objection that wage restraint seriously violated trade union interests (despite its sympathy for the government's arguments). In turn, the powerful personalities on the General Council helped to implement the agreement successfully by projecting their strong fear that the failure of wages freeze might precipitate a return to depression conditions with its attendant problem of mass unemployment.

43. Lord Williamson and Lord Geddes interview, see *nn.* 32, 41.

Conservative Government: Failure of Wages Bargaining, 1956

T HE 1948 wages bargain demonstrated that government efforts to manage the economy since 1945 had thrust such producer groups as the TUC into vastly more powerful roles as bargainers with government over the formulation and implementation of economic policy than ever before. But it showed also that the nature of the relationship between a major producer group and the political party in office could decisively affect the conduct and outcome of that bargaining, and that producer group power thus was subject to important limitations and restraints.

The Labour government successfully used its close personal, organizational, and ideological relationship with the trade union movement at the climactic moment in the 1948 negotiations to force an agreement with the TUC against the will of the General Council.

The Conservative party's reformulation of its economic policies after the war, especially its management of the economy after 1951, thrust the Tories into a bargaining relationship with the TUC over the terms of economic policy. In 1956–1957 the Conservative government tried to conclude an agreement for wage restraint with the TUC in response to the second severe balance of payments crisis in the postwar era. In contrast to the 1948 example, the negotiations failed because the TUC was able to exercise a veto against the Conservative proposals. Uninfluenced by any bonds of loyalty, the General Council could more freely decide to give or to withhold its cooperation. The government headed by

Anthony Eden did not have the advantage of close relationships with the TUC which Labour had used to force an agreement in 1948. Therefore, the course and outcome of bargaining for wage restraint in 1956 depended far more on the successful resolution of substantive differences than it had with Labour. In sum, in 1956, with a Conservative government in office, the TUC was a more powerful spokesman producer group.

The TUC, however, exercised only negative power that was focused entirely on the outcome of the negotiations. During the course of these negotiations, each side was virtually deaf to its opponent's counter arguments and strategies, thus reflecting the traditionally stiff, formal, and often unfriendly relations between trade unionism and the Conservative party. Further, each side found it particularly difficult to compromise on the issue of wage restraint. The government urgently needed to slow inflation; effective wage restraint was the only feasible alternative to its imposition of severe deflationary measures. The TUC, on the other hand, refused to consider any wage restraint agreement that did not provide generous compensating subsidies, as well as social and economic benefits—which the government invariably found unacceptable. In addition, the newer leaders on the General Council were increasingly impatient with any collaboration that compromised trade unionism's right to pursue freely the benefits of full employment. This stress on the primacy of trade union interests was expressed in the veto that the TUC delivered against wage restraint at the end of the negotiations. The government, in response, chose to impose the deflationary alternative rather than to engage the TUC and the trade union movement in a bitter and possibly disastrous struggle over legislated wage restraint.

CONSERVATIVE REFORM TOWARD THE MANAGED ECONOMY

The Conservative party moved decisively to accept the concept of the managed economy during its six years in opposition and four years in power in the decade between 1945 and 1955. By 1955 it had closed most of the distance between its views and those of Labour about economic policy. This change, which J. D. Hoffman and other authors attribute to the resurgence of the traditional Conservative will-to-win after their severe and surprising defeat in 1945, gave economic policy throughout the decade a striking continuity. Conservative governments perceived economic problems and solutions in much the same way Labour governments had. Thus, Conservative governments also were dependent on their relationships with competing producer groups for the success of their economic policies.

The Conservatives began to reformulate their economic policies in earnest after the 1945 election. Labour's overwhelming victory shocked the Conservative party because Churchill's prestige had been expected to be the decisive factor in its favor regardless of the issues. In defeat, however, many in the party quickly came to agree with R. A. Butler that the Tories had failed to win because the memories of the depression were still strong and because they had failed to offer a positive alternative to Labour's proposals.[1] The job, as Butler saw it, was to formulate an alternative. Within a few months after the election, Churchill appointed Butler to head the party's Research Department and to conduct an examination into Conservative policy.

The Industrial Charter, published and approved by the party during the spring of 1947, was the most significant economic policy document produced by that examination. The *Charter* pledged the party to a new course in economic policy based on the positive value of the state's management of the economy. It specifically called for "strong central guidance" in developing economic strategy and in using fiscal policy to implement that strategy by controlling the level and balance of economic activity. To accomplish this, the *Charter* accepted the role of the unbalanced budget; a stiff, sharply graded income tax; and even the principle of na-

---

1. Butler, *Fundamental Issues*, p. 2.

76 CHAPTER 5

tionalization in certain industries, including power, transportation, and the Bank of England.

The *Charter* marked a sharp turn for the Tories. In a word, it significantly narrowed the economic policy differences between the parties. Labour's deemphasis of physical planning during the government's last three years in office, coupled with the Conservatives' implementation of the terms of the *Charter* after they regained power in 1951, demonstrated that the remaining differences were barely perceptible.

The similarities between the stewardships of Butler as the Conservative and Hugh Gaitskell as the Labour Chancellor of the Exchequer were so striking that *The Economist* dubbed their common policies "Butskellism."[2] Butskellism was "an interesting mixture of planning and freedom based on the teachings of Lord Keynes."[3] Its principal concern was the aggregate level of demand based on the total amount spent on goods and services. When the economy was sagging, as defined by a rising level of unemployment and a slowing down of the rate of production, government would step in and by inflating the budget, lowering taxes, and/or lowering interest rates, take the lead in putting more purchasing power into the economy. On the other hand, when the economy was overheating (as demonstrated by price inflation, a worsening balance of payments, and perhaps a very high level of employment), government would remove purchasing power from the economy by using the same instruments in the opposite direction.

Tables 5.1, 5.2, and 5.3 illustrate the continuity between Labour and Conservative economic policies since the war. Butler kept Conservative election promises to reduce taxes and to remove controls and restrictions. His "bonfire of controls," however, was really a continuation of a process that Gaitskell had begun in 1950 but halted because of the Korean War and accompanying rearmament program. Even

2. *The Economist* (February 13, 1951), p. 440.
3. Brittan, *Steering the Economy*, pp. 112–113.

TABLE 5.1. EFFECT OF DIRECT ECONOMIC CONTROLS, 1946–1956 (Percentage Controlled)

Type of Controls	Labour Govt. 1946	Labour Govt. 1948	Labour Govt. 1950	Conservative Govt. 1952	Conservative Govt. 1954	Conservative Govt. 1956
Extent of consumer rationing (not weighted)[a]	28	31	11	10	6	2
Extent of import controls[b]	96	91	73	65	34	16
Extent of price controls[c]						
Tightly controlled	32	35 (1949)	34	24	11	8 (1958)
Loosely controlled	16	14 (1949)	11	4	None	None

Sources:

[a] Dow, *The Management of the British Economy*, table 6.3, p. 173, citing *National Income and Expenditure of the United Kingdom* (Treasury, London: H.M.S.O., 1957, 1959, and 1960). Percentage of expenditures controlled.

[b] Ibid., table 6.4, p. 174, citing M. F. W. Hemming, C. M. Miles, and G. F. Roy, "A Statistical Summary of the Extent of Import Control in the United Kingdom Since the War," *Review of Economic Studies*, 26 (February, 1959), 75. Percentage of imports purchased by government or subject to government restriction, weighted by value of imports in 1955.

[c] Ibid., table 6.6, p. 176, citing Dow, *National Income and Expenditure of the United Kingdom*, annual reports. Percentage of expenditures controlled.

TABLE 5.2. TAX LEVELS, 1938–1959 (Percentage of GNP)

Type of Tax	Conservative Govt. 1938	Labour Govt. 1946	Labour Govt. 1951	Conservative Govt. 1959
Personal Income Employment Income	1.1	5.6	4.8	5.1
Dividends, Interest, Rent, Trading Income	4.6	6.5	4.4	3.5
Corporate Income	1.8	7.4	5.8	4.6
Capital	1.5	1.6	1.5	1.0
Expenditures	8.0	14.6	14.8	11.9
TOTALS	16.9	35.8	31.4	26.1

Source: Dow, *The Management of the British Economy*, table 7.1, p. 188, citing Dow, *National Income and Expenditure of the United Kingdom*.

TABLE 5.3. BALANCE OF PAYMENTS, 1948–1956

Year	Net Balance of Payments of the United Kingdom on Current Account (£m)
1948	7
1949	38
1950	297
1951	− 419
1952	227
1953	179
1954	204
1955	− 92
1956	192

Source: Butler and Freeman, *British Political Facts 1900–1967*, p. 227.

so, Butler proceeded only slowly and cautiously when he resumed the "bonfire." In 1954, three years after coming into office, the Conservative government still maintained controls on more than one-third of all imports; price controls on about 10 percent of all items; and taxes at only slightly lower levels. The Tories were cautious about removing controls, it should be noted, even though Britain was enjoying comparatively excellent years of balance of payments surpluses that totaled more than £600 million (see Table 5.3). Thus, Conservatives, who had so loudly criticized Labour in 1951 for maintaining high taxes, physical controls, and import restrictions were most reluctant in practice to remove these restrictions, even in a time of comparative national prosperity.

This convergence and continuity between Tory and Labour economic policies meant that the Conservative government by 1955 viewed economic problems and their solutions much as the Attlee government had. This was demonstrated in 1955 and 1956 when the Eden government made the decision to deal with its first economic crisis by almost precisely the same methods that the Attlee government had employed in 1947–1948.

THE ECONOMIC CRISIS OF 1955

The causes of the economic crisis of 1955 are found, as they have been in so many postwar British economic crises, in the excesses of the prosperity that preceded it. From the beginning of 1952 until the middle of 1954 the world trade situation was extraordinarily favorable for Britain. The prices of raw materials, so important to British industry and so high during the Korean War, declined. In 1953, the annual bill for British imports was about 25 percent lower than the bill of two years earlier. At the same time, British exports edged upwards. The net effect of this radical turnabout in world trade was to give Britain several hundreds of millions of extra pounds to spend on foreign and domestic commodities, including food, then becoming much more plentiful in the world markets. Moreover, the rapid increase in consumer spending between 1952 and 1954 occurred without any significant price inflation. Sizeable increases in productivity (5 percent in 1953 and 6 percent in 1954, using 1948 as the standard) allowed the supply of goods to expand almost as rapidly as the purchasing power.[4]

The official outlook in early 1955 was exceedingly optimistic as Anthony Eden succeeded Winston Churchill and prepared to call an early election. To fuel the continued expansion, the government submitted a pre-election budget in April, 1955, that provided for the largest tax reductions in more than nine years. Businessmen, who had continued to be quite cautious about the strength and viability of the economic boom up to that moment, took the expansionary budget as the signal to begin making long-delayed investments in new plants and equipment in order to increase their already strained productive capacity. Throughout the spring of 1955 the pressure of orders, particularly for such hard goods as cars and heavy machinery, continued to grow at a rapid pace and employment reached record levels.

---

4. Treasury, *Economic Survey 1956,* Cmd. 9728 (March, 1956), p. 16.

Problems were beginning to develop, however, just at the moment when things looked most optimistic. Prices for raw materials began to turn upward at the end of 1954. At the same time, growing labor shortages and rising corporate profits were creating enormous pressure within many unions for large wage increases. These changes, coupled with a perceptible leveling of the rise in productivity, triggered a new round of inflation in the spring of 1955. The pre-election budget of April served to stimulate the inflation and push the economy into a very difficult balance of payments situation.

The boom soured very rapidly and the signs of trouble were clear by the early summer of 1955. But the government did not explicitly recognize them until the end of that summer. *The Economist* put the blame for this turn of events squarely on what they saw as the irresponsibility of trade union leaders in making unreasonable wage demands. It recommended that the government invoke a strong dose of deflation based on a rate of unemployment that would establish an "equilibrium" to stabilize wage levels.[5]

Butler's departure from the Treasury during the fall of 1955 left the problem to his successor as chancellor, Harold Macmillan. The alternative policies, as the government viewed them, were to impose a kind of tough deflation (as proposed by *The Economist*) that would involuntarily restrict spending in large measure by creating a much higher level of unemployment, or, to try to resurrect the kind of voluntary price and wage restraints that the Labour government had been able to put into effect in 1948.

The imposition of a tough deflationary policy, although the most efficient way to cool the economy, posed the politically unpleasant consequences of high unemployment and stifling controls. Also, neither side of industry would accept state-imposed directives on wages and prices. Macmillan, therefore, had to find a solution that would continue full employment, stabilize prices and wages, dampen business

---

5. *The Economist* (August 20, 1955), p. 596.

investment without choking it off, and otherwise cool the economy as gently as possible.[6]

The conclusion of a wage-price agreement was the most essential and difficult task. The Labour government had achieved wage restraint only after prolonged negotiations and the application of intense pressure on the TUC. The Conservative government, on the other hand, might grasp the opportunity to use the Conservatives' close relations with business to obtain agreements for price restraint, but wages agreement undoubtedly would be considerably more difficult.

TORY GOVERNMENT AND THE TUC

The chances that Macmillan could convince the General Council to accept a new period of wage restraint initially seemed promising because of the exceptionally good relations that the Churchill government had developed with the TUC over the prior four years. The critical question for the Eden government was whether these good feelings represented a fundamental change in trade union-Conservative relations that could be transferred from the Churchill to the Eden government. The improved relationship turned out to be nontransferable.

Winston Churchill, his Minister of Labour Walter Monckton, and, to a lesser extent, R. A. Butler were the architects of the unprecedented good feelings between the Conservative government and the trade union movement between 1951 and 1955. The government's management of the economy preserved and reinforced the importance of the TUC in the political process. Like the Labour government before, the Conservatives freely and continuously consulted with and asked for the cooperation of the TUC on virtually all issues related to the problems of wages, productivity, employment, and on economic policy in general.

---

6. Eden, *Full Circle, The Memoirs of Anthony Eden*, p. 363; Macmillan, *Tides of Fortune: 1945–1955*.

Churchill told Monckton (in unmistakable language) to make certain no major strikes occurred: " 'Winston's riding orders to me were that the Labour Party had foretold grave industrial troubles if the Conservatives were elected, and he looked to me to do my best to preserve industrial peace.' "[7] Monckton followed his instructions to the letter, often enduring sharp criticism from within his own party that he was selling out to the unions. He made a special effort to understand union interests and to be conciliatory, especially on wages. His success in winning the confidence of trade union leaders is reflected in the fondness with which many union leaders still remember him.[8]

The character and tone of the relationship was set soon after the Tories returned to power. The rearmament program, initiated in 1950–1951 in response to the Korean War, had contributed to a very serious balance of payments problem and an accompanying domestic price inflation. On one front, the new Churchill government wanted to find a way to slow the rate of wage increases (though not necessarily a freeze as the government would try to accomplish in 1956). Chancellor of the Exchequer R. A. Butler therefore met with the General Council in April, 1952, to see whether the TUC would agree to try to tie wage increases more closely to increases in productivity—also a familiar Labour government theme.[9] The General Council reacted sharply, replying that the council could not agree to this proposal so long as the government insisted on reducing subsidies and adding insurance charges while doing nothing to restrain prices and profits.

Discussions between the Prime Minister, the Chancellor, and the General Council and the Economic Committee[10]

7. Birkenhead, *Walter Monckton*, p. 276.
8. Fred Jones, former member of the TUC's Economic Department and Assistant Secretary with the Department of Economic Affairs. Interview, July 14, 1969.
9. Trades Union Congress, *Report of Proceedings, Annual Trades Union Congress* (1952), p. 284.
10. "The Economic Committee, which consists of 15 members of the Gen-

of the TUC dragged on fruitlessly from the middle of April until August. No agreement was reached, nor was there any real progress toward an agreement. The government's only attempt to force the issue was the rejection of a batch of Wages Council recommendations for wage increases in July. When the TUC vigorously protested this action to the Prime Minister, however, Churchill immediately reassured the General Council that the government would settle the claims during the following month; he also assured the council that he meant the "reference back" only as a "gesture" of the government's resolve to strengthen the country's economic position.[11]

The end of the talks in August without agreement and the settlement of the wage claims on TUC terms set the pattern for the relationship during the balance of Churchill's incumbency. Churchill and Monckton carefully avoided major strikes for four years by influencing wage settlements in trade unionism's favor and by keeping to a minimum government's demands for union cooperation on other controversial issues.[12] This strategy successfully produced an era of good feelings but did little to alter fundamentally the relationship between trade unionism and the Conservative party because Churchill's approach was based on an explicit policy of conflict avoidance.

The period of good feelings between the TUC and the Conservative government ended with the departure of Churchill and Monckton in 1955. The succeeding Eden

---

eral Council, meets regularly once a month, but more often when necessary. The committee deals with both general and specific matters relating to economic and industrial developments. Among the very wide range of subjects which fall within its competence, . . . [are] . . . prices and incomes policy, . . . international trade, developments in the European Economic Community and the European Free Trade Area, . . . and the submission to the Government of a statement on the economic situation and the Budget." Trades Union Congress, *Trade Unionism*, p. 8.

11. Trades Union Congress (1952), p. 293.

12. George Woodcock, former Chairman of the Commission on Industrial Relations and former General Secretary and Assistant General Secretary of the TUC. Interview, July 17, 1969.

government had to make insistent demands for TUC cooperation in order to deal with the growing crisis. These demands, in turn, sharply clashed with a new militancy developing within the trade union movement.

The TUC and its constituent unions in 1955–1956 were
undergoing an important shift in attitudes and leadership.
The distasteful experience of the 1948–1951 wage restraint,
plus the experience of a booming prosperity between 1952
and 1954, spawned a new militancy within many unions.
This had an important effect on the composition and, in
turn, the policies of the General Council beginning in 1955.
Younger men, who had gained support for their rise to
leadership by their promises to give primacy to trade union
interests, succeeded the more conservative leaders, who were
the staunchest advocates of collaboration with governments
of either party in the name of "national interest."

The most striking and most publicized of these changes
occurred in the largest and most powerful union, the Transport and General Workers. From the beginning of the Second World War until his death in 1955, Arthur Deakin
used his position as General Secretary of the Transport
Workers to build a majority on the General Council in favor of strong and consistent cooperation with the government-of-the-day. Deakin argued that the development and
maintenance of a strong economy with full employment was
the prerequisite for union strength from which good collective bargaining agreements could be negotiated.[13] Frank
Cousins, who became General Secretary after Deakin, criticized this sort of collaboration. He insisted that the first
responsibility of any trade union leader was to try to get what
his men wanted.[14]

Other new leaders, such as Jim Campbell of the Railwaymen and Alan Birch of the Union of Shop, Distributive,
and Allied Workers, gave the General Council a new complexion by early 1956. The council did not turn uncom-

---

13. Allen, *Trade Union Leadership*, pp. 149–150.
14. Trades Union Congress, *Report of Proceedings, Annual Trades Union
Congress* (1956), p. 400.

promisingly toward militancy in 1956. Rather, it became much more cautious and a bit antagonistic about everything which smacked of collaboration against the primary interests of trade unionism. The General Council was eager to gather the fruits of full employment, and less concerned about how to avoid another depression.[15]

NEGOTIATIONS

The more intransigent attitude of the General Council toward collaboration on economic policy and the fundamental hostility of trade unionism toward the Conservative party clearly made the government's task in developing a new agreement on wage restraint more difficult in 1956 than Labour's task in 1948. Unlike Labour, the Conservative government had no ideological, organizational, or personal ties that it could use as leverage to pressure the TUC to agree. Thus, the TUC could choose to veto Conservative economic policies. Agreement between the TUC and Conservative government depended on the successful resolution of differences through the formal negotiating process, which was exactly the reverse of the TUC's relationship with the Attlee government. In 1948, the TUC exercised influence on the course of the negotiations by delaying, as well as seeking, compromises to Labour's policies, but, at the end point, TUC leaders felt helpless to resist Labour's pressure to agree. The Conservative government in 1956, however, would have had to make many more policy concessions to win TUC support for a wages agreement than their Labour predecessors had had to make in 1948. The course of the negotiations in 1955–1956 showed that the Eden government was not prepared to pay this price.

The government's strategy for achieving wage stability

15. Len Murray, Assistant General Secretary of the TUC and formerly head of the TUC's Economic Department from 1948 until 1969, commented in an interview on July 31, 1969, that the General Council in 1955 began to take the critical view that TUC leaders had been too easily satisfied during the first postwar decade.

clearly acknowledged the weakness of its position in dealing with the TUC. Rather than approaching the TUC directly as Labour had done in 1948, the Eden government chose instead to appeal first to the business community for price restraint.[16] A Conservative government, the Cabinet reasoned, would more easily win business cooperation for price stability than union cooperation for wage restraint. Price stability, once achieved, might then be used as a powerful argument in favor of an agreement on wages. This seemed to be a rational argument, especially in view of the TUC's increasing concern with giving primacy to trade union interests. The General Council had often made price stability one of the prerequisites for collaboration.[17] The kind of economic policy demanded by the employers' organizations in return for their agreement on prices, however—including reductions in government spending and a government supported drive against restrictive trade practices—so alienated the General Council, which had long called for expansionary policies, that any agreement on wages became more difficult to achieve.

The negotiations for price and wage restraint passed through three phases from October, 1955, until the Suez crisis of November, 1956. During the first phase, from October, 1955, through February, 1956, the government concentrated on winning the support of the business community through the employers' organizations. After gaining a number of promises from individual firms on price stability, Eden and Macmillan began discussions with the TUC in March, 1956, in an effort to trade price stability for agreement on wages. These talks, which lasted into June, were unproductive. Finally, in the third phase, the government made a last effort to win agreement from the TUC by extracting even firmer and more widespread commitments on price stability from private enterprise, as well as from the nationalized industries. These efforts collapsed because the General Council and then the annual Congress rejected any

---

16. Eden, loc. cit.
17. Trades Union Congress (1956), p. 263.

form of wage restraint, and thereby effectively ended the whole project. In frustration, the new Macmillan government in 1957 adopted many parts of the tough deflationary alternative that the government had rejected two years before.

October, 1955–February, 1956. The first phase in the government's efforts to win price-wage stability went very well, as it acted to soothe employers' fears of a runaway inflation. In October, the Chancellor submitted a second budget for the year containing a number of deflationary measures designed to reduce demand moderately. These measures reversed the April tax reductions and removed £113 million per year from the economy, primarily by raising purchase taxes substantially. Then, four months later in February, 1956, the government tightened the squeeze even further:

1. The bank rate was raised to 5½ percent.

2. Various steps were taken to reduce private and public investment, including a cut of £50 million in the investment plans of the nationalized industries.

3. Tighter controls on credit agreements were imposed.

4. Subsidies on bread and milk were reduced by a total of £38 million per year.[18]

These measures pleased the business and financial community. Throughout the fall the British Employers' Confederation (BEC) and the Federation of British Industries (FBI) applauded the government's actions.[19] The BEC, on its own initiative, tried to convince employers to withhold price increases. By December a number of firms had announced their intention of holding their prices steady for a fixed period, usually six months. In January and February, 1956, Prime Minister Eden repeatedly praised these actions and exhorted other firms to follow suit.

---

18. House of Commons. *Parliamentary Debates,* vol. 548 (February 17, 1956), cols. 2675–2681.
19. Federation of British Industries, *Annual Report,* pp. 3–4.

March, 1956–June, 1956. Armed with vocal business support and a growing number of commitments for voluntary price freezes by private firms, the Prime Minister invited the General Council to meet with him about the economic situation on March 5, 1956. The General Council had voiced increasing criticism of the government's actions to restrain inflation in reports published by the TUC's Economic Committee in November, 1955, and February, 1956.[20] The TUC objected very strongly to the government's "excessive" and "indiscriminate" use of monetary policy to produce a financial squeeze that they charged was having its most direct effect on the working people who were less able to cushion themselves against transitory economic pressures. For the same reasons the TUC objected to purchase tax increases, income tax increases, and especially the additional reductions in housing and food subsidies. The General Council argued that the government's policy of "deliberately dismantling the machinery of control and planning in order to return to a freer economy, coupled with measures which have resulted in the redistribution of income, has given rise to fears in the minds of many workpeople [*sic*] that their standards of living are in danger."[21]

The General Council repeated these charges in the meeting with the Prime Minister on March 5. The council agreed with the government that the economic situation was serious and that the logical solution would be to reduce the level of consumption and investment. Council members suggested, however, that the government selectively impose restrictions in both the public and private sectors only on less essential investments. They urged, however, that investments on socially related capital projects such as schools, hospitals, and housing, be continued. Also, they argued that imports of unessential commodities should be directly limited. Taxes should be increased on profits and high incomes, while tax concessions for the poor should be raised. Finally,

20. Trades Union Congress (1956), pp. 258–263.
21. Ibid., p. 262.

purchase taxes on fuel and essential items should be lowered and building licenses be limited.[22]

The General Council indicated that the government would have to give favorable consideration to these proposals if there were to be serious discussions about trade union cooperation with the government's economic policies. Nevertheless, after the meeting council spokesmen told reporters that they had heard nothing to stir them to cooperation.

Neither the publication of the White Paper on the economic situation, *The Economic Implications of Full Employment,* a few days after the first talks, nor a further discussion between the General Council and the Chancellor on March 27 did anything to move the parties toward any sort of agreement.[23] The White Paper merely restated the government's position and failed to offer any new proposals or suggest that the government would take firm action on wages. The second meeting was totally fruitless and at the end the General Council flatly told the Chancellor, "Wage claims would continue to be pressed so long as the cost of living was rising."[24]

The deadlock in the talks at the end of March, 1956, offers an interesting contrast to the discussions between the TUC and the Attlee government in November, 1947. Unlike the Labour government, the Conservatives stated their position explicitly and indicated what they wanted very clearly and repetitively. Labour had been quite vague and hesitant in stating demands for TUC collaboration before that government broke the deadlock by taking unilateral actions which led to a settlement that the TUC felt the trade union leadership could not refuse. In March, 1956, the TUC simply refused to accept the government's clear prescriptions for the economic problems which the TUC acknowledged were real and serious. The questions before the government in face of this deadlock as the Conservatives prepared to submit their budget in April, 1956, were whether

---

22. Ibid., pp. 262–263.
23. Cmd. 9725 (March, 1956).
24. Trades Union Congress (1956), p. 263.

they should attempt to entice the TUC into agreement by
modifying their policies, or, failing that, whether they could
do anything, as Labour had, to force an agreement.
The April, 1956, budget was therefore an important
bench mark in the negotiations. The government firmly decided not to meet the TUC's criticisms in order to attempt
to win the General Council's support for wage restraint.
Instead, Macmillan tailored the budget to reinforce his appeal to business for support on price restraint, in turn, as an
inducement to the TUC for wage restraint. The budget
further tightened the squeeze by reducing government expenditures, in part, by ending the bread subsidy which the
TUC had contended was so important. The employers' organizations commended the budget as demonstrating the
government's commitment to meet inflation head on by reducing public expenditures. The General Council, on the
other hand, was sharply critical and the union attitude in
the discussions hardened considerably.[25] The budget served
to weaken seriously the already diminishing forces on the
council in favor of collaboration.

The additional talks between Macmillan and the Economic Committee during May were totally unproductive
and caustic. In a speech at Newcastle-upon-Tyne on May 25
Macmillan signaled the end of this phase of the negotiations
and stated the government's frustration and anger with the
TUC. For the first time, Macmillan in this speech publicly
blamed rises in wages and salaries for price inflation. He
warned that additional price inflation would dry up new export orders, which, in turn, would make it difficult for
Britain to continue to import necessary food and raw materials. To this, Frank Cousins replied tartly the following
day:

> We are not very impressed by his [Macmillan's] telling us
> that if there are no wage increases for 12 months everything will
> be all right. . . . There is a Government in power at the mo-
> ment that is determined, if it can, to create a situation in which

25. Ibid., p. 265.

our bargaining power is less than now. The method is by creating
a situation in which we are not so anxious to challenge them
because there may be a man waiting around the corner for the
job.[26]

By early June, therefore, the negotiations had broken
down almost completely. It was at a similar point in February, 1948, that the Labour government had abruptly issued the White Paper condemning any further increases in
wage levels which subsequently broke the deadlock in the
negotiations with the TUC. The striking difference in 1956
was that at no time did the Conservative government hint
nor the TUC fear that the trade unions would be coerced to
agree.

The Conservative government was reluctant to break
the deadlock by taking unilateral action, as Labour had done,
because of the fear that these measures would produce an
open hostility that could precipitate an even more serious
crisis. Lacking the influence that the Labour government
exerted, the Conservatives could expect solid opposition
from the General Council which was much less worried, after
years of full employment, that council opposition would precipitate a new depression. This attitude would make it very
difficult to implement any government action or legislation
against a movement so vast and diffuse. Finally, the General
Council's anger at a Conservative government's arbitrary attempt to break the deadlock might well have spilled over to
produce a paralysis in the myriad of industrial issues that
daily are the subject of consultations and otherwise routine
cooperation. The government in 1956 instead almost immediately retreated from Macmillan's tough words to make
what was a last try for a voluntary agreement based on price
stability.

July, 1956–September, 1956. The employers' organizations
had continued to be as pleased as the TUC was displeased by

---

26. *The Times* (London), May 28, 1956, p. 7.

the government's economic policies, particularly the cuts in
government spending that were announced in the April
budget. The Chancellor had met throughout the spring
with the representatives of the FBI and BEC as frequently
as he had met with the TUC. These meetings had gone well
and generally it was agreed that the government was following a correct approach in cooling off the economy, although
the employers were not enthusiastic about the increase in the
profits tax and suspension of the investment allowance.[27]
When the talks with the TUC broke down in early June,
however, Macmillan decided to put his good relations with
private enterprise to better advantage by moving more force-
fully to develop a firmer "prices plateau." He still thought
this was the best and perhaps the only way to convince the
General Council to make any effort on wages.

At a meeting on June 11, Macmillan and Prime Minister Eden explicitly asked the BEC and the FBI to step up
their drives to convince their members to make specific
commitments for a lengthy prices freeze.[28] The spokesmen
for the two organizations replied that although they were
sympathetic to the Prime Minister's request, they were concerned about recent price increases announced by some of
the nationalized industries. They felt their members were
most eager to support the government but that they would
have to have firm assurances the public sector would hold
the line as well. The Prime Minister replied he would immediately attempt to get such assurances.

During the following two weeks Macmillan met sepa-
rately with the heads of all of the nationalized industries. By
the end of June he had won their public commitments to
refrain from further price increases for a period of twelve
months in most cases. Then, after several additional meetings, the employers' organizations indicated they were ready
to endorse the "prices plateau." At a joint press conference
on July 22 they announced that because the government had

27. Federation of British Industries, *Annual Report*, p. 4.
28. *The Times* (London), June 12, 1956, p. 10.

reduced public expenditures and the nationalized industries had promised to hold their price levels for the coming year they were recommending that their members in private enterprise take similar actions because ". . . the time had come when private industry should play a like part. . . ."[29]

Price stability was achieved over the succeeding months, which was a considerable accomplishment. As a strategy to influence the TUC, however, it failed completely. The General Council continued adamantly to refuse to make any agreement on wage restraint. On August 1, the government recognized that its efforts had failed by announcing the talks were being suspended. In three short separate meetings that evening with representatives of the TUC, the several employers' organizations, and the heads of nationalized industries, the government repeated its position and obliquely scolded the unions:

> The Government must . . . emphasize that the national interest can be served only by a continuing effort to keep prices steady and if possible reduce them, even where this process would affect profits and dividends. All those responsible for wages questions should show a similar recognition of the national needs.[30]

The TUC delivered a final answer one month later at Congress. By unanimous consent and after angry and emotional speeches criticizing the government, Congress shouted approval of a resolution decisively rejecting any form of wage restraint:

> Congress asserts the right of Labour to bargain on equal terms with Capital, and to use its bargaining strength to protect workers from the dislocations of an unplanned economy. It rejects proposals to recover control by wage restraint, and by using the nationalized industries as a drag-anchor for the drifting national economy.[31]

---

29. Federation of British Industries, *Annual Report*, p. 4.
30. *The Times* (London), August 2, 1956, p. 8.
31. Trades Union Congress (1956), p. 528.

CONCLUSION

The negotiations for wage restraint in 1956 failed because the TUC and the Conservative government were unable to resolve their policy differences. The General Council, influenced by new militancy within its ranks, refused to agree to wage restraint based on the proposals put forward by the Eden government. The government, for its part, was unwilling to meet General Council criticisms by adjusting its proposals to spur the negotiations toward an agreement. Instead, implicitly recognizing their weak position with trade unionism, the government chose the more indirect strategy of seeking support for price restraint. It then hoped to trade price restraint (or a "prices plateau," as it came to be known) to the unions for wage restraint. The Conservative government had no means, however, to force an agreement after the TUC refused this trade. On the other hand, the TUC, frustrated in its efforts to influence Conservative policy substantively, was effectively able to exercise a veto on it.

The TUC's veto also reflected its growing anger over its inability to influence the Eden government's economic policies in general, and, too, its distrust of all agreements with the Tories, especially one on so vital an issue as wage restraint.[32] Policy frustration, therefore, provided a convenient rationale for vetoing the whole scheme. The TUC's refusal to recognize the government's successful efforts to achieve price restraint as providing a basis for wage restraint, after it had said repeatedly that a halt to rising prices was a necessary precondition to successful negotiations, indicates that the General Council probably never really intended to agree anyway.

The Conservative government's efforts to reach an agreement with the TUC for wage restraint therefore contrasted significantly with the Labour government's efforts eight years earlier. In 1948 the TUC exerted its strongest influence on the course of the negotiations. However, the TUC acquiesced reluctantly but meekly when the Labour

---
32. Flanders, *Trade Unions*, p. 167.

government pressed most intensely for the final agreement. The reverse was true in 1956. The TUC was unable to influence the course of the negotiations. Yet, when the Conservative government pressed most intensely for an agreement, the TUC stubbornly held its ground and brought the discussions to an end, thereby effectively vetoing wage restraint. The Conservative government could have forced agreement by legislating wage restraint. It did not. This would have alienated the TUC and forced a serious confrontation which might have jeopardized both the implementation of wage legislation as well as the administration of existing laws and policies that required trade union cooperation.[33]

The contrasts in the 1948 and 1956 examples relate most strongly to the differences in the relationships between the TUC and the two parties, and, in turn, to the effects that they have on the decision-making process within the TUC.

The double-edged effects of the close ties between the TUC and the Labour party caused the hesitant and uneven process by which the two sides stumbled to an eventual agreement. The dilemma for the General Council in 1948 was whether to reject wage restraint and give primacy to trade union interests or whether to collaborate with the government, "their government," in the national interest. At the decisive moment, the pressure for collaboration from "their government" won the day.

The absence of close ties between the TUC and the Conservative party meant that the General Council faced no comparable dilemma in choosing between collaboration and conflict. This freedom from obligation was the key to its exercise of a veto at the climactic point in the bargaining process. The TUC could much more easily and objectively appraise Conservative economic policies and decide ques-

---

33. Some of the economic subjects that the TUC cooperated on with the government in 1956–1957 were: import duty policy, housing policy, occupational pension schemes, a committee to investigate the workings of the monetary and credit system, a committee to investigate agricultural marketing, and coal distribution cost problems.

tions about union cooperation on their merits, giving primacy to union interests. Internally, such independence greatly eased tensions and conflicts within the General Council and between the TUC and its constituent unions and allowed the TUC to operate from a substantially stronger bargaining position.

The persistent problem for the TUC in 1955–1956, as in 1947–1948, was that it exerted influence on economic policy in a purely negative manner. With the Labour government, the TUC exerted its influence on the course of the bargaining by causing the government to hesitate and delay its actions; with the Conservative government, it vetoed agreement at the end point in the bargaining. In neither case did the TUC successfully influence the government to adjust its own policies nor accept alternatives proposed by the TUC.

Conservative Government
and the Problem of Pluralistic Stagnation:
Pay Pause and "Neddy,"
1961

THE deadlock in the 1956 negotiations demonstrated that a danger of the new group politics might be not "oppressive efficiency but rather pluralistic stagnation."[1] Pluralistic stagnation is a situation in which government has found it impossible to win producer group acceptance of its policies, and the consequence of that failure is inaction or, more specifically, the immobilization of policy. Thus, pluralistic stagnation is both an unanticipated and dangerous outcome of producer group politics which points up government's difficult task in convincing the leaders and members of producer groups to "adjust their own behavior to the requirements of its programs."[2]

The consequence of pluralistic stagnation in 1956 was continued economic stagnation. The development of widespread interest in planning during the late fifties was stimulated by growing concern with the inability of producer groups and government to create a stable and prosperous economy. When Britain faced yet another economic crisis in 1961, the Conservative government headed by Harold Macmillan boldly tried to avoid renewed deadlock with the TUC by imposing a wages freeze or "pay pause" without TUC consultation in the public sector in the hope that private enterprise would then follow its example. At the same time,

---

1. Samuel Beer, "The British Legislature and the Problems of Mobilizing Consent," in *Lawmakers in a Changing World*, Elke Frank, ed., p. 38.
2. Ibid., p. 39.

97

the Chancellor of the Exchequer, Selwyn Lloyd, attempted
to negotiate the creation of an economic planning mechanism to spur economic growth and to provide a forum by
which the government could mobilize producer group consent. The government's strategy failed, however, because it
seriously miscalculated the intensity and effect of trade
unionism's reaction to the pay pause. The TUC viewed the
pause not only as an arbitrary, unjust assault on the amounts
in its members' pay envelopes, but, more importantly, as a
brazen attempt by the Tory government to redefine the
terms of industrial relations in order to diminish the TUC's
influence on economic decision making. Together with the
union rank and file whose anger was focused on the wages
issue, the General Council successfully defeated the pay
pause.

The TUC thus opted to risk continued pluralistic stagnation with economic failure rather than to compromise its
power or policies. It finally agreed to join the planning organization, the National Economic Development Council
(NEDC or "Neddy"), after the government officially ended
the pause. But it so qualified the terms of its participation
that Neddy became the institutionalized re-creation of the
pluralistic stagnation that the government had sought to
overcome.

FROM STAGNATION TO PLANNING

Both the TUC and the government shared the view in
1956 that, deadlock aside, the economic situation was serious
and in need of remedial action. Blocked from implementing
the most crucial portion of its anti-inflation program, the
government imposed severe deflation by raising the bank
rate, lowering public expenditures, and increasing taxes.
This "second-choice" approach worked poorly. Deflation
took hold during 1957, but quickly passed into a recession,
and in 1958 the government hurried to reflate while the

TABLE 6.1. UNEMPLOYMENT

Year	Thousands	Percentage of Estimated Total Number of Employees
1957ᵃ	312.5	1.4
1958ᵃ	457.4	2.1
1959ᵃ	475.2	2.2
1960		
January	460.6	2.1
April	391.2	1.8
August	321.4	1.4
December	365.0	1.6

Source: Central Statistical Office. *Monthly Digest of Statistics.* July, 1961, table 30, p. 25.
ᵃ Monthly averages.

TABLE 6.2. WAGES AND PRICES, 1957–1960

Year	Wages January 31, 1956 = 100	Retail Prices January 17, 1956 = 100
1957ᵃ	110.0	105.8
1958ᵃ	114.0	109.0
1959ᵃ	117.0	109.6
1960		
January	118.3	109.9
April	119.6	110.3
August	120.4	110.4
December	122.2	112.2

Source: Central Statistical Office. *Monthly Digest of Statistics.* July, 1961, table 167, p. 138 and table 169, p. 140.
ᵃ Monthly averages.

TUC complained bitterly about the almost doubled rate of unemployment.[3] (See Table 6.1.) The reflation worked well enough to contribute to the reelection of the Tory government in October, 1959. However, by 1960, prices and wages were rising rapidly again and the balance of payments was falling into another round of deficits. (See Tables 6.2 and 6.3.) The cycle of boom and bust, caustically dubbed "stop-

3. For a concise review and analysis of the course of Conservative economic policy from 1956–1960, see Dow, *The Management of the British Economy*, pp. 90–111. For the TUC's angry reaction to the 1957–1958 recession, see the speech by William Carron, a member of the General Council and president of the powerful Amalgamated Engineering Union to the 1958 TUC Congress, Trades Union Congress, *Report of Proceedings, Annual Trades Union Congress* (1958), pp. 419–420.

TABLE 6.3. BALANCE OF PAYMENTS—Current Account (£m)

Year	First Quarter	Second Quarter	Third Quarter	Fourth Quarter
1958	+127	+83	+89	+21
1959	+20	+75	+19	−24
1960	−44	−50	−136	−109

Source: Central Statistical Office. *Monthly Digest of Statistics.* December, 1961, table 142, p. 112.

go" by Labour party leader Harold Wilson, was again complete. Pluralistic stagnation thus contributed to Britain's continued record of dismal economic failure.

The economy's backslide into trouble in 1960 provoked widespread concern with these recurring problems. Sharp criticism was directed at institutions and groups involved in the conduct of economic activity and, especially, at the "blundering" government and the "obstructionist" trade unions.[4] Unfavorable comparisons between Britain's chronic problems and the uninterrupted decade of economic growth of her European neighbors, the vigorous promise incited by the Kennedy election campaign in the United States, and the reaction to the Conservatives' boastful 1959 election promises that prosperity was finally here to stay, all contributed to these feelings. The image of Britain as a tired, old-fashioned nation was very much in vogue.

In response to and proceeding from their own concerns, organized business, the TUC, the Treasury, members of the academic community, the media, and several independent research organizations began a broad and largely uncoordinated search for solutions to Britain's economic stagnation. "Economic growth" was the key term in the debate.[5] The development of a high and sustained growth rate was pinpointed as a goal which, if achieved, would finally allow for increasing standards of living, stable prices, a surplus in the

4. A most provocative and influential book published during this period was Shanks, *The Stagnant Society.*
5. Probably the most influential book in stirring interest in the concept of economic growth in Britain during 1960–1961 was Political and Economic Planning, *Growth in the British Economy.*

balance of payments, and a strong currency, maintaining, all the while, full employment.

The surge of interest in indicative economic planning was most particularly concerned with the problem of pluralistic stagnation. Indicative planning meant the government's concern with the formulation of certain objectives for the economy; an analysis of the ways in which these objectives could be reached; and predictions about the course of economic activity over the next period of years.[6] It was concerned also, as drawn from the French planning experience, with the problem of how to improve intra-societal communications so as to influence economic, political, and social decisions in order to achieve stated objectives. Compulsion by government was not part of this definition. Rather, planning was voluntary and government worked in harness with those groups who performed the "productive function" under the disciplined examination of a joint, deliberative council. Group politics, as related to economic policy, would, if planning were adopted, therefore begin to operate within a regular institutional setting where issues were more sharply focused, and disagreements would be resolved, it was hoped, by the give and take of comprehensive bargaining.

Both the government and the TUC found a host of advantages in this concept of economic planning. A rapidly growing, prosperous, and stable economy would clearly serve all interests. Both the TUC and the government also noted that economic planning might work to their strategic and substantive advantage. For example, the Chancellor of the Exchequer, Selwyn Lloyd, noted that the government might be able to develop TUC support for a permanent incomes policy in the planning council.[7] He also reasoned the existence of an "educational" value for the TUC in being constantly exposed to the "broader implications" of government's actions. Most importantly, he believed the TUC

6. Authorities disagree as to the precise definition of economic planning. This broad but comprehensive definition is drawn from Henderson (ed.), *Economic Growth in Britain*, chap. 7.
7. Selwyn Lloyd, member of Parliament and former Chancellor of the Exchequer. Interview, July 23, 1969.

would find it more difficult to play a consistently intransigent role while participating in council decision making.[8] In sum, the Chancellor hoped that the Conservative government would be able to gain crucial access to and influence with trade unionism in order to blunt the TUC's well-demonstrated negative power.

For its part, the TUC General Council hoped to develop positive influence on Conservative policy by participating in planning work.[9] Specifically, the council was eager to influence Conservative economic policy before it was publicly announced.[10] Internally, the TUC hoped to enhance its authority vis-à-vis its constituent unions by virtue of the work of its representatives on the planning council who would be in a position to make decisions on major economic questions that would directly affect the interests of each union.[11]

Several studies capably analyze how the enthusiasm of first business, then labor, and finally prominent officials in the Treasury influenced the government to propose the creation of a planning mechanism.[12] Brittan and Christoph both give credit to the employers' organization, the traditional defenders of the status quo, for providing the lead on planning. The Federation of British Industries (FBI) in November, 1960, sponsored a conference concerned with the future of economic activity in Britain, the report of which was titled "The Next Five Years." Businessmen, government officials, a few economists, but no labor leaders attended the conference. The most important result was the report of the subgroup headed by Sir Hugh Beaver, a leading business executive, whom Brittan characterizes as an "industrial radical." Contradicting the prevailing government view, the Beaver group boldly argued that "the achievement of a faster

8. Ibid.
9. George Woodcock, former Chairman of the Commission on Industrial Relations and former General Secretary of the TUC. Interview, July 17, 1969.
10. TUC Economic Committee, "The Purpose in Joining The N.E.D.C.," p. 1.
11. Woodcock interview, n. 9.
12. Brittan, *Steering the Economy*, chap. 6; and Christoph, "The Birth of Neddy," in *Cases in Comparative Politics*, Christoph, ed.

growth rate might be the best way of achieving stable prices and a sound balance of payments, and not the other way around."[13] The best way to achieve economic growth, the report declared, was to plan for economic development, taking into account the French experience.

The FBI conference generated a good deal of excitement and discussion at the Treasury and at the TUC. In January, 1961, the TUC's Economic Committee authorized its staff to make a complete study of the possibilities for planning. Within the Treasury, Sir Edward Boyle, Financial Secretary to the Treasury, and Professor Alec Cairncross, the government's newly appointed chief economic advisor, were the most important officials pressing the case for planning. A number of conversations about planning took place during the winter of 1960–1961 between Cairncross, Boyle, and Selwyn Lloyd and, in turn, between Lloyd and Macmillan, who had a long-standing interest in planning.[14]

The government finally proposed the creation of a planning mechanism on July 25, 1961.[15] Selwyn Lloyd was convinced by then that planning would be a highly useful approach for solving Britain's economic problems. He chose, however, to use the announcement that the government planned to begin talks about creating a planning mechanism with both sides of industry, to soften his decision to impose severe deflationary measures, including a wages freeze or "pay pause" in the public sector in order to deal with Britain's sixth postwar economic crisis.

Lloyd's first concern was to solve the crisis that suddenly deepened and intensified during the spring of 1961. The immediate cause of the crisis was the revaluation of the German and Dutch currencies in March, and the rush by speculators to sell sterling. Coming on top of continuing balance of payments deficits, Selwyn Lloyd saw this wave of speculative selling as a clear signal that the government would have

13. Brittan, p. 150.
14. Ibid., p. 151.
15. House of Commons. *Parliamentary Debates*, vols. 645–646 (July 25, 1961), cols. 218–229.

to act quickly in order to save the integrity of the pound.[16] In his April budget, he raised taxes and took authority to adopt "tax regulators" which he could impose if the situation grew worse. By July, however, the drain on British reserves was reaching what he felt were alarming proportions and he prepared much more drastic measures.

The government hoped to overcome pluralistic stagnation in 1961 and prevent its recurrence in the future.[17] The pay pause was part of that approach. Unlike earlier efforts to develop wage restraint or freeze, the government arbitrarily and without consultation, imposed a wages freeze in the public sector which was not subject to prior veto by the unions. In turn, the government hoped its example would convince private enterprise to impose its own wages freeze and thus slow inflation without the need for another round of fruitless and paralyzing negotiations with the TUC.

For a permanent solution, Lloyd sought to establish a planning council as quickly as possible. It was through the work of the council that he expected to ease trade union intransigence to government economic policies by bringing the TUC closely into the economic decision-making process.

NEGOTIATIONS

The General Council initially accepted Lloyd's invitation to participate in the talks on economic planning in order to use that forum to press him on the wages issue.[18] Secondarily, the council was interested in finding out specifically what sort of planning proposal the Chancellor had in mind.

The Economic Committee, charged with the negotiating responsibility, met with Selwyn Lloyd for the first time on August 23. The pay pause was by then beginning to upset

16. Lloyd interview n. 7.
17. Lloyd interview, n. 7; he commented he had hoped to forestall a repeat of the 1956 deadlock.
18. TUC General Council, "The Government's Economic Measures," p. 5.

the well-advertised plans of the Railwaymen and other public-employee unions to submit new and substantial claims. Their anguished complaints prompted the committee at a private preliminary meeting to harden its strategy.[19] George Woodcock thus opened his remarks to Lloyd by bluntly warning that the TUC would not agree to participate in economic planning work until the government ended the pay pause. He emphasized that the TUC would continue to hold this position even though it strongly favored planning and might find the government's proposals appealing.

Selwyn Lloyd, in response, merely shrugged off Woodcock's warning by reiterating that the government intended to persevere with the pause because it was absolutely necessary.[20] The present discussions, he said, were intended to be distinctly separate from his measures to deal with immediate economic problems. Therefore, Lloyd added, he hoped the Economic Committee would lay aside its disapproval of the pause during the negotiations in the interest of reaching agreement on planning. He promised, moreover, that if these negotiations proved fruitful, the TUC would have a genuine chance to influence economic policy in the formative stage—although the government would, of course, always retain the ultimate responsibility for economic policy.

He proceeded to outline two alternative proposals for economic planning machinery.[21] The first proposal was for a wholly independent planning body that would simply prepare a national economic plan. The second, which he said he favored, was for a national economic council, with twenty to twenty-five members chosen from the trade union movement, private business, and the government, plus some independent members. The government members would be the Chancellor, who would act as the chairman of the council, and probably the President of the Board of Trade and the

19. TUC General Council, "Meeting Between Economic Committee and Chancellor," p. 1.
20. Ibid., p. 2.
21. Trades Union Congress, Report of Proceedings, Annual Trades Union Congress (1962), p. 252.

Minister of Labour. The council, as the supreme policy-making body, would have a full-time staff that would be totally independent of the government, although it would have free and continuous access to the resources of the various departments and ministries. Members of the staff would be drawn from the civil service, and would serve two- or three-year assignments with the planning organization. The staff's primary task would be to produce correlated forecasts of industrial growth, particularly as they related to specific industries, and to analyze obstacles to growth for each of those industries.

The members of the Economic Committee were pleased with the Chancellor's preliminary ideas on planning. They felt that a representative council would provide a good forum in which the TUC could influentially state its views on economic policy. In contrast, however, the Chancellor's brusque rejection of George Woodcock's complaints about the pay pause indicated that the government would not compromise its position, regardless of TUC threats to withhold cooperation on planning. The main struggle over the pay pause therefore shifted to the shop floor where the local unions in the private sector sought to destroy the credibility of the freeze in the public sector by winning continued wage increases.

The outcome of the planning negotiations in London thus became bound to the struggle over the pay pause on the shop floor during the fall of 1961. Formal and informal negotiations between the government and the TUC continued into October and November, while both sides kept anxious eyes on the temperature of industrial relations and the latest figures on changes in wage rates. Selwyn Lloyd sent his formal proposal for the creation of the National Economic Development Council (NEDC or Neddy) to the TUC and the employers' organizations on September 23. TUC leaders generally approved of Lloyd's proposals, but they had several important reservations. The members of the Economic Committee wondered whether they could believe the Chancellor's promise to consider seriously the Neddy Council's advice in reaching policy decisions in view of his action to impose the pay pause without consultation.[22] Also, the committee worried that the government intended to use the council only to push for a permanent incomes policy, but otherwise choke off discussions about issues the TUC might want to raise. Therefore, the committee insisted that Neddy's decisions be recommendations rather than directives and that all council members be free to bring up any issues. Also, they insisted that trade union representatives be strictly accountable only to the TUC for their appointment, removal, and the views they expressed.

The government, eager for agreement, quickly accepted all these conditions. The attitude of the Economic Committee and the nature of the conditions, however, pointed up the important change in the TUC's view of Conservative planning since Lloyd imposed the pay pause. The committee was, by the fall, much more concerned that planning not be used against them, rather than with the advantages that trade unionism might gain. It felt that the Neddy proposal was part of a wider Tory effort to prevent the trade union movement from decisively influencing issues that directly or indirectly affected its interests. The Economic Committee therefore became determined to build trade union veto power into TUC participation on the Neddy Council.[23]

The government's persistence with the pay pause during the fall added to the TUC's anger and distrust. Despite indications that the number of unofficial strikes was increasing and that wage inflation was continuing unabated in the private sector, Lloyd held fast to his view that the pause must go on until productivity had a chance to catch up. To the

---

22. *The Times* (London), October 26, 1961, p. 12. "The TUC insisted that anything in which they took part should have some effect. What they had to decide now, on the basis of what the Chancellor had told them, was whether there was a reasonable chance that the Government would pay attention to what the new council said."
23. Lord Douglass, member of the Electricity Council and former member of the General Council and Chairman of the TUC Economic Committee. Interview, July 15, 1969.

TUC's dismay, the government on October 6 announced it would reject the claims for 2 shillings a week by 120,000 members of the Transport Workers and General and Municipal Workers Unions. At about the same time, the government also announced it would pay only 8 shillings of a £-a-week increase granted by an industrial court in January to a number of civilian workers in the admiralty. Neither personal protests to the Prime Minister nor the Economic Committee's repeated postponements of planning negotiations budged the government from its position. On November 14, the Economic Committee sent a letter to the Chancellor restating its position on the pause and urging him to reverse himself before the chances for planning disappeared and the country, under the weight of misguided deflation, fell into an even more serious economic crisis.[24]

Then, two days after the Economic Committee sent its letter, the Electricity Council agreed to pay an overall increase of between 5 and 8½ shillings to all its employees beginning January 28, 1962. The General Council hoped this would provide the crucial blow against the pay pause. Council members speculated that perhaps the government had acquiesced in the action and was signaling that it planned to change its position. *The Times,* in an editorial on November 20, commented, "with the government's pay pause apparently in ruins, attention during the coming weeks may shift to the possibility of a more long-term policy. . . ."[25] The article added that "other industries, whether public or private, will no longer feel under the same obligations to resist claims to keep in line with the Government's policy."[26]

24. The TUC's Economic Department, the staff arm of the Economic Committee, was genuinely alarmed about the prospects of a recession. In a paper prepared for the Economic Committee at the end of November, the department pointed out that the sharp fall in industrial production since July, the fall in retail stocks and retail sales, the much smaller increase in employment and the marked increase in short-time working which took place in October indicated that a recession in economic activity was rapidly developing. TUC Economic Committee, "Recent Economic Developments," pp. 1–2.
25. November 20, 1961, p. 10.
26. Ibid.

Prime Minister Macmillan strongly refuted this speculation on the following day in Parliament. Rather than confirming the end of the pause, Macmillan scolded the Electricity Council for granting the award, and reaffirmed the government's determination to continue the pause:

While there has been some improvement as a result of our short-term policies the economic situation remains serious. . . . I must, therefore, urge all concerned . . . to maintain a policy of restraint over wages, salaries, and dividends.[27]

TUC leaders were surprised by the strong tone of the Prime Minister's denunciation of the Electricity Council's award and his vigorous defense of the pay pause. The members of the Economic Committee had been confident that the government would soon recognize the futility of continuing the pause. The October figures showed a sharp increase in the weekly wage bill as compared to the same month in 1960; and there was a growing number of potential strikes brewing, as well as actual and serious strikes in the aircraft industry and on the docks. In a private paper, the Economic Committee told the General Council that such a pause as there had been was applied only to national wage agreements, while wage increases continued to be conceded in the plants. The committee added it was very doubtful whether, when the pause came to an end, it would have had *any* restraining effect on rises in incomes.[28]

Publicly, the General Council castigated Macmillan's speech and announced it would suspend further consideration of joining Neddy. The Economic Committee asked for an early meeting with Selwyn Lloyd to discuss the whole matter.

Lloyd met with the Economic Committee on November 28, a week after the Prime Minister made his statement.

27. House of Commons. *Parliamentary Debates,* vol. 649 (November 21, 1961), cols. 1145–1147.
28. TUC Economic Committee, "The Government's Wages Policy," p. 2.

The TUC representatives were angry and Harry Douglass
sharply told the Chancellor that his renewed insistence on
this "misguided" policy had undermined the General Council's confidence in his word. Further, he said, the government's position was astonishing since it was clear that the
pay pause was breaking down as trade unionists learned they
could gain wage increases by threatening to strike. George
Woodcock then added that the Chancellor did not seem to
entertain the possibility that the government's analysis might
be in error, thus demonstrating a rigid attitude that was the
very antithesis of consultation. He warned Lloyd further
that if the government continued to hold its current position
on the pay raise there was little point in the TUC's joining
Neddy.[29]

In response, Lloyd startled the committee by telling
them he was considering alternatives to the pay pause—perhaps a "guiding light" principle, for example—that would
relate wage increases to productivity. He added that any
alternative form of incomes policy would also have deficien-
cies but that the government intended to consult with both
sides of industry in early 1962 about a new approach. The
Chancellor then again emphasized he hoped the pay pause
dispute would not prevent cooperation in solving the more
fundamental problems of the economy, particularly because
he had carefully included TUC views in his planning proposals.

The November 28 meeting proved to be the crucial
turning point in the negotiations. The government had
clearly changed its mind between the day that Prime Minister Macmillan scolded the Electricity Council and the day,
a week later, when Lloyd met with the Economic Committee.
The evidence was overwhelming that trade unionism was
defeating the pay pause on the shop floor. The TUC's angry
reaction to the Prime Minister's statement indicated the General Council would determinedly press that defeat as far as

---

29. TUC Economic Committee, "Meeting between the Chancellor and Economic Committee," pp. 2–3.

necessary. Further, the rash of unofficial strikes and threatened strikes was providing solid evidence for the Economic Committee's warning that union men would oppose the pause regardless of whatever action their leadership might take.[30] Therefore, with the pay pause in shambles, the government decided that its most urgent priority was to save the planning proposal.

The immediate creation of the Neddy Council offered the best chance to solve current problems and would allow the Conservative government a chance to deal more effectively with trade union power in the future. The Economic Committee, with strong assistance from the membership had, in sum, enforced its demand that the government end the pay pause as the TUC's price for joining Neddy.

The strategic consequences of the November 28 meeting played heavily on the balance of the formal and informal negotiations. The next formal meeting between the Chancellor and the Economic Committee was not held until January 5, but important informal and tacit bargaining took place in the intervening month.

The first substantive public break came a little more than a week after the November 28 meeting. The Home Office allowed a substantial pay increase for firemen to take effect on January 1. Despite the official explanation that the increase had been granted because it had an "element of pre-pause commitment," *The Times* commented that "the rise of technical niceties . . . will certainly not prevent workers elsewhere from observing that very large increases have been given to members of a public service in the middle of a pay pause."[31]

George Woodcock responded one week later by announcing an important shift in the TUC's position on joining Neddy. Speaking to the Glass Manufacturing Federation on December 12, Woodcock announced that the TUC just might decide to join Neddy despite its feelings about the

---

30. Ibid., p. 2.
31. *The Times* (London), December 9, 1961, p. 9.

pay pause and the government's general handling of economic policy.

> I think the movement is going to be faced with the question
> . . . whether we shall allow what I consider understandable resentment at the rather peremptory, obdurate attitude of the Government in relation to the pay pause to be the decisive factor when considering the question of long-term planning.
> It would, in my view and in the view of a majority of my colleagues, be wrong for the T.U.C. to allow peevishness, resentment, however justified to be the decisive factor in the decision to be made.[32]

Then in a speech to the House of Commons on December 18, Selwyn Lloyd publicly confirmed that the government intended to replace the pay pause. While affirming the original necessity and value of the pause, Lloyd said that it was now time to begin discussions with both sides of industry about replacing the pause with an intermediate plan which would still provide some restraining influence on the growth of incomes but allow for small salary increases. In this same speech he announced the formal creation of the planning staff, to be headed by Sir Robert Shone as Director-General.

Thus, the basis and momentum for a final agreement were well developed by the time that the Economic Committee again met with the Chancellor on January 5. The Economic Committee posed two additional questions to the Chancellor and pressed its advantage in the negotiations to get "satisfactory" answers. They wanted to know on what date the pause would end, and exactly what the government meant by the next or intermediate phase in wages policy. They added, however, that regardless of what the Chancellor had in mind, the Economic Committee was not prepared under any circumstances to commit themselves or the General Council to any proposals which restricted the right of unions to attain the highest possible wage increases for their members.[33]

---

32. Ibid., December 13, 1961, p. 6.
33. TUC Economic Committee, "Meeting between the Chancellor and Economic Committee," p. 1.

The Chancellor did not answer these questions immediately, but promised to send the TUC a formal, written reply in a few days.

The Chancellor sent his answers in a public letter to the Economic Committee on January 10. The pay pause, he said, would end on March 31—at the end of the fiscal year.[34] He asked, however, that the TUC and the employers' organizations agree to arrangements for the pay pause to be replaced by a "guiding light" principle that would provide a form of restraint during 1962. He further suggested that the "guiding light" be defined as a limit of 2½ percent per year in wage increases. Turning to the question of planning, he again asked for the TUC's participation in Neddy.

The Economic Committee was satisfied that the government would not attempt to push wage restraint very hard in the future. Therefore, the committee recommended to the General Council that it agree to join Neddy. The General Council accepted this recommendation on January 24. At the same time, the General Council took careful pains to reject ". . . all the possibilities put forward by the Chancellor for restraining wages during an 'interim' period after the end of the pay pause."[35]

The government announced the "guiding light" in a White Paper issued on February 2, 1962. The General Council responded with a short press release simply referring to its statement of January 25, rejecting the concept.[36] The government took no public notice of the TUC's statement, nor any action to enforce the "guiding light," and the first meeting of the Neddy Council was held on March 7, 1962.

CONCLUSION

The immediate outcomes of the 1961–1962 struggle were, on the one hand, the TUC's defeat of the pay pause

---

34. For the text of the Chancellor's letter to the Economic Committee, see *The Times* (London), January 11, 1962, p. 6.
35. Trades Union Congress (1962), p. 244.
36. *Incomes Policy: The Next Step*, Cmnd. 1626, February, 1962.

and, on the other, the Macmillan government's success in establishing Neddy. However, the Conservatives again had to adopt growth-stifling alternative fiscal and monetary measures in order to reduce demand, and, because of the conditions the TUC demanded for its participation, Neddy institutionalized the pluralistic stagnation it was supposed to remedy. Thus, the ultimate result of the government's efforts to solve the problem of pluralistic stagnation in 1961 was renewed pluralistic stagnation.

Selwyn Lloyd seriously underestimated the force of the wages issue within the trade union movement when he adopted the "tactic" of tying his announcement of the pay pause with his proposal for planning. He thought he could have both. He knew the TUC would be unhappy about the pause but he reasoned that the appealing prospects for planning would blunt their opposition. Instead, the TUC made planning a virtual hostage in its successful fight to kill the pause. The Economic Committee's initial interest in planning as a vehicle for achieving positive influence in the formation of Conservative economic policy gave way to a highly defensive concern with protecting the status quo. The committee became concerned that the planning council not become an instrument for Conservative economic oppression.

The two most important reports that the Neddy Council published during the remaining two and one-half years of Conservative administration reflected the fundamental stalemate. At its second meeting in May, 1962, the council authorized the preparation of a comprehensive report on the implications of an average growth rate of 4 percent for the following five-year period. That report, *Growth of the United Kingdom Economy, 1961–1966,* was published in February, 1963. A second, follow-up report, *Conditions Favourable to Faster Growth,* was published a few months later. Both reports suffered, however, from their failure to analyze thoroughly the issues related to economic growth or to offer concrete solutions for the problems they identified. Wage inflation was considered only briefly.[37] This superficial and inconclusive treatment of the wage issue reflected the deadlock on the council. Progressively, the council bogged down in squabbles, and tempers on all sides grew quite short as the 1964 election approached.

The struggle in 1961 was thus more complex than the immediate disagreement over the pay pause and wage restraint policy. It was rooted more in the question of the TUC's future influence on economic decision making and in what the General Council viewed as a threat against the basic right of the trade union movement to seek the best possible terms of employment for its members. The government had sought to mitigate the power of the TUC to use its dissent as a veto which could dangerously paralyze policy. By defeating the pay pause and leaving Neddy a victim of pluralistic stagnation, the TUC reversed the government's challenge and reinforced its influence on economic decision making. However, this outcome significantly diminished the prospects that the Conservative government could solve Britain's economic problems. For the TUC demonstrated it was not prepared to fulfill the consequences of its own long-standing demands for economic planning, because, in reality, the demands clashed with the fundamental purposes of trade unionism. Successful economic planning required that the TUC compromise its interests in order to develop a workable policy and neither the TUC nor its constituent unions and members were prepared to pay this price. Instead, they continued jealously to guard their power to pursue the advantages of full employment.

---

37. See especially the section "Power and Incomes," pp. 48–51.

Crisis and Change in the
Trades Union Congress:
The Ineffective Alliance with Labour,
1964–1967

HAROLD WILSON led the Labour party to victory in the 1964 election, in part on the promise that Labour would deal more effectively with critical economic problems than the Tories had. He pledged that a Labour government would be able to enlist effective union cooperation for wage restraint, without fear of stalemate, in order to help achieve a high and sustained rate of economic growth.

In contrast, the Wilson government's management of the economy and relationship with trade unionism were strewn with disappointments. Severe and unexpected balance of payments crises intruded in each year between 1964 and 1967. In response, the government urgently sought trade union cooperation for progressively more stringent wage restraint. The TUC reluctantly agreed to collaborate as it had in 1948, again honoring its traditional loyalties to the Labour party. However, in contrast to 1948, the General Council was not able to implement wage restraint because its decisions to collaborate opened a serious breach in the union movement. A large and growing number of union leaders, including a minority on the General Council, and especially shop stewards and rank and file members on the shop floor, strongly opposed the council's actions because they compromised their rights to bargain for the best terms of employment. In 1964 and 1965 they registered their strong disapproval of the General Council's leadership by ignoring the wage restraint agreements. Instead, they successfully continued to win wage increases in the factories, increases that were above the rates established in national settlements.

This rise in militancy was rooted in the convergence between the economic programs of Conservative and Labour governments since 1945. Despite their continuing political allegiance to Labour,[1] trade union leaders were coming to assess economic policy more pragmatically. The long years of full employment, even under Conservative governments, had blunted their once potent fear of renewed depression.[2] They now argued vigorously that the first responsibility of the TUC was to insist on the primacy of trade union interests in its relationship with government. Militancy thus diminished the ability of the TUC to reach and effectuate agreements with governments of either party that impinged on those interests. In turn, policy became ever more susceptible to dangerous paralysis as government continuously extended its management of the economy and its corresponding need for TUC cooperation.

COLLABORATION AND DISUNITY

Prime Minister Wilson made his government's most significant economic decision on the day he took office, when he decided not to devalue the pound despite finding that Britain was facing an unprecedented balance of payments deficit of perhaps £800 million in that fiscal year.[3] He decided against devaluation because he felt it would only briefly gloss over, rather than solve, Britain's fundamental economic problems. Wilson was also sensitive to the Conservatives' success since devaluation in 1949 in tagging Labour as the

1. Goldthorpe et al., *The Affluent Worker: Political Attitudes and Behavior*, p. 73.
2. James Mortimer, member of the National Board for Prices and Incomes and former General Secretary of the Draughtsmen's & Allied Technicians' Association. Interview, August 5, 1969.
3. Brandon, *In the Red*, p. 31.

"devaluation party," with all the implications of economic deprivation that that label implied.[4]

Once made, Wilson's personal decision not to devalue, coupled with Labour's earlier commitment to avoid "Tory-style stop-go" deflation while trying to achieve a high and sustained rate of economic growth in the context of economic planning, meant that the Labour government faced a constricted range of policy alternatives—as long as the government continued to place the integrity of the pound alongside the maintenance of full employment as competing goals of economic policy. The requirements for solving both short-term problems and developing long-term growth conspired to place maximum stress on government efforts to develop an immediate, comprehensive, yet permanent, incomes policy.

The two central figures in the relationship between the new government and the Trades Union Congress on economic policy were George Brown, the Deputy Prime Minister and Secretary of State for Economic Affairs, and George Woodcock, the General Secretary of the TUC. Brown was a logical person to carry the heavy responsibility for economic affairs and particularly for dealing with the trade unions. As chief deputy to Wilson in the government as well as in the Labour party, Brown spoke with considerable authority. As a former official of the Transport and General Workers Union, Brown had a broad and deep range of contacts within the union movement. He was immensely popular with virtually every member of the General Council and held their confidence as "one of us."[5]

Brown headed the Department of Economic Affairs (DEA), which the new government established to be the comprehensive economic planning agency in the government. The DEA was created by the transfer of almost the entire staff from Neddy's Economic Division; its purpose was to do the kind of economic planning that Neddy had been do-

4. Ibid., pp. 31–32.
5. Lord Douglass, member of the Electricity Council and former member of the General Council and Chairman of the TUC Economic Committee. Interview, July 15, 1969.

ing, but to do it *inside* the government. Neddy was retained as an independently functioning agency, but the Labour government, committed to intervene more vigorously in managing the economy, wanted to take the lead in planning. Under Labour's reorganization, Neddy would continue to operate as the focus for tripartite negotiations on economic policy, and especially on the questions and problems of removing specific obstacles to growth, but Neddy would not be expected to formulate planning policy. Instead, the Labour government opted to do its own planning and to present its proposals to the Neddy Council as recommendations in search of support. Unlike the Tories, Labour already counted on union support and saw no reason why it needed to yield the planning function to the Neddy Council. The Labour government much preferred to deal with the TUC on a private, informal basis. The Cabinet worried little at this point, as the Tories had done, about the problems of policy stalemate and the use of Neddy as a vehicle for the resolution of intractable disagreements.[6] They proceeded to create the DEA, in fact, with the approval and enthusiastic support of the TUC's Economic Committee.[7]

The DEA's major responsibilities were to prepare a *National Plan*[8] and to oversee the development of an effective prices and incomes policy to make possible the effective implementation of the plan.

---

6. Fred Jones, Assistant Secretary, Department of Economic Affairs and former member of the TUC's Economic Department. Interview, July 14, 1969.
7. Douglass interview, see *n.* 5.
8. The *National Plan*, published in September, 1965, was described by George Brown in his "Foreword" as "a guide to action" for British economic development between 1964 and 1970. Its main goal was to increase national output by 25 percent during that period in order to solve permanently the balance of payments problem and to achieve a rapid and stable rate of economic growth. The plan defined obstacles to growth and established specific production goals for the whole range of individual industries. It was officially abandoned in July, 1966, however, when the government imposed severe deflationary measures to deal with its third balance of payments crisis. Before that, the plan had been subjected to an enormous amount of public criticism for being, among other things, too hastily prepared, unrealistic in its targets, devoid of concrete recommendations for realizing the goals it set, and contradictory in the context of the government's parallel pledge not to devalue the pound.

The rapport that Brown enjoyed with the General Council members as a whole did not extend, however, to his relationship with George Woodcock. An introspective and intellectual man, Woodcock's personality contrasted strikingly with the mercurial and ebullient Brown. Woodcock had been an honors fellow in economics at Oxford and had spent nearly all of his more than three decades in the trade union movement at the TUC. Before he became General Secretary in 1960, Woodcock had been Assistant General Secretary under Vincent Tewson for fourteen years, and before that had headed the TUC's Economic Department for eight years. He was not well liked by most of his colleagues. They found him cold and aloof and not very interested in the rough and tumble of trade union politics. But they did respect him immensely for the clarity of his thinking and his intense loyalty to the interests of the movement.

Woodcock's influence as General Secretary never equaled that of Walter Citrine. He did achieve, however, an extraordinary control over the TUC's economic policies, due in good measure to his unquestioned understanding of economics and the forcefulness of his views. His interest in economics sometimes even precluded his attention to other TUC business, but in the changed relationship between trade unionism and government since the end of the war, his command of economics gave him a strong position of authority.

The clash between Brown and Woodcock, as it developed between 1964 and 1966, went beyond the difference in their personalities. George Brown laid a good share of the blame for Britain's chronic economic problems on the slothfulness and obstructionism of a massive trade union movement, represented by a TUC that was understaffed, underpaid, and overworked, though technically competent.[9] He made these criticisms of trade unionism quite openly to his friends on the General Council in a way that would have aroused howling anguish if they had been said by a Conservative minister. The way to get action from the trade union movement, Brown contended, was to give the unions "fre-

9. Douglass interview, see *n*. 5.

quent kicks in the shins," in order to prod and scare the General Council into action.[10]

Woodcock agreed that the trade union movement was allergic to change,[11] but not that "a kick in the shins" would prod the movement into action. Demands for specific action under a barrage of threats would be counterproductive, he argued. Instead, government policy should be used to evoke understanding and a willingness to change within the unions. The more crucially an issue impinged on the central purposes of trade unionism, i.e., wages, hours, working conditions, the longer and more difficult would be the struggle to change established union attitudes. He therefore felt the government or the General Council, for that matter, could develop an effective incomes policy only through a long, slow, educative process. Woodcock stood as a transitional figure in the trade union movement. His views contrasted markedly with the outright collaborationist views of his predecessor as General Secretary, Vincent Tewson, but he was far more dedicated to finding areas of agreement with the government than some of the more militant, younger trade union leaders. He played a decisive role in the TUC's relationship with the Labour government in extracting concessions where he could, but he was quick to recognize the responsibility he felt to reach agreements with the government when he thought it needed legitimate help or when he thought that the trade union movement stood to lose more than it could gain by intransigence. He was even more aware, however, of the increasing limitations that the General Council faced in getting the rank and file to give effect to its agreements.[12]

Wages, Prices, and Productivity Agreements, October, 1964– April, 1965. Less than a week after the election Brown

10. Fred Catherwood, Director-General of the National Economic Development Council. Interview, June 26, 1969.
11. Woodcock, *The Trade Union Movement and the Government*, p. 19.
12. George Woodcock, former Chairman of the Commission on Industrial Relations and former General Secretary of the TUC. Interview, July 17, 1969.

bluntly told George Woodcock privately that the government
wanted and "desperately needed" an incomes policy in order
to deal with the serious economic situation it had found
upon taking office, and as part of its long-term plan for
achieving economic growth and eliminating the seemingly
endless series of balance of payments crises.[13] Woodcock, in
reply, said that if the situation really were that grave, he was
sure the General Council and, in turn, the whole movement
would accept a short-term freeze or period of severe restraint
rather than risk the even uglier possibilities of deflation with
accompanying high unemployment or outright devaluation
with a sharply higher cost of living.[14] He warned, however,
that any sort of freeze would begin to deteriorate the same
day it was imposed and could not be effective for long, perhaps no longer than a few weeks. He suggested instead that
Brown consider developing a longer-term comprehensive and
voluntary incomes policy that would help less in the present
situation but would give the government a much better
chance to make its plans for expansion work.

The full General Council then met with the Prime
Minister for the first time on October 26, the day that the
government issued its first White Paper on the economic
situation. The White Paper pointed out the existence of
the serious balance of payments problem that the new government had "inherited" but confidently declared that the
government would be able to deal successfully with the problem.[15] The only significant remedial measure announced in
the White Paper was a 15 percent surcharge on imports—a
nondeflationary action. The General Council unanimously
agreed to announce publicly its support for the White Paper
and to applaud the use of the surcharge to restrict the flow of
imports.[16] The council also agreed to the Prime Minister's
request to begin discussions on an incomes policy and to
participate in the drafting of the *National Plan.*

---

13. Trades Union Congress, *Productivity, Prices, and Incomes: Report of a
Conference of Executive Committee held on 30th April 1965*, p. 31.
14. Ibid., pp. 32–33.
15. *The Economic Situation, A Statement by Her Majesty's Government*, October 26, 1964.
16. Trades Union Congress, *Report of Proceedings, Annual Trades Union
Congress* (1965), p. 283.

The government was in the meantime preparing its first budget, which it then introduced in November. Although it imposed major new taxes on corporate incomes and capital gains, it noticeably refrained from increasing personal taxation and both raised welfare benefits and abolished prescription charges—thus redeeming two long-standing Labour promises. The TUC was pleased with these actions, and readily renewed its pledge of full support and cooperation.[17] London and International financial interests, however, were considerably less enthusiastic and viewed the budget as a sign that the Labour government intended to follow an anti-business policy, and would be more interested in redeeming its social commitments than fulfilling its obligations to protect the value of the pound. Two days after the budget was introduced, this erosion in confidence was translated into a wave of selling in sterling. Selling continued to increase daily until November 23 when the government finally acknowledged the seriousness of the situation by raising the bank rate by two full points, from 5 to 7 percent. Two days later the Bank of England announced that a consortium of banks including the United States Export-Import Bank had agreed to provide £3 billion in credits upon which the government would be able to draw in the event the run on the pound continued, or any subsequent crises arose.

The massive loan and the increase in the bank rate helped to ease the pressure on the pound. However, it did not bring selling back to "normal" levels. The government's actions in the crisis were comparatively mild but they did represent a first deflationary step, openly designed to reassure the international financial community. Forced by circumstances, the government had resorted to the use of monetary instruments that would have a dampening effect on investment during the coming year. High interest rates would discourage new investment. An increase in the bank rate by itself did not significantly jeopardize the credibility of the government's plans to promote economic growth, but to the TUC it was a symbolic "first chink" in that policy. Since the TUC's support was predicated in good measure

17. Ibid., pp. 283–284.

on the government's adherence to economic expansion, re-
trenchment from expansionism prejudiced that support.
The first faint signs of strain, of misgivings, appeared in December, 1964, and January, 1965. TUC staff economists began to caution the Economic Committee that the Prime Minister and the Chancellor had been badly shaken by the
sterling crisis and were becoming ever more anxious to cater
to the international financial community in order to forestall future crises.[18]

The negotiations between the TUC, the government,
and the employers' associations, which had been going on
for about two weeks when the sterling crisis erupted, took
on a sense of urgency under George Brown's prodding after
the government raised the bank rate. The conversation between Brown and Woodcock and the approval of the General Council on October 26 had led very quickly to full-scale
negotiations for a long-term, comprehensive, three-part
agreement on prices, wages, and productivity. Brown had
taken George Woodcock's advice and decided to forego an
immediate wage and price freeze in favor of a gradual, voluntary policy whose effect would be most relevant to the
goals for economic growth to be expressed in the *National
Plan*.[19] The first stage of the agreement was to be a Declaration of Intent—a statement by the three sides accepting the
concept of voluntary restraint on wages and prices with wage
increases tied to gains in productivity. The General Council,
still eager to help the government, agreed to sign the declaration in December.

In January, the General Council first questioned the
government's apparent interest in deflationary measures as
an appropriate response to balance of payments problems
and sterling crises. The council warned the government it
should avoid imitating the Tories:

. . . [T]he underlying problem of achieving a substantial
and continuing improvement in the balance of visible trade still

18. David Lea, staff member of the TUC's Economic Department. Interview,
July 10, 1969.
19. Trades Union Congress, *Productivity, Prices, and Incomes*, p. 33.

remains unsolved. What has been proved by experience is that deflation of demand does not automatically increase exports. The remedy has been tried and has failed too often.[20]

The council members were worried about the direction that Labour policy seemed to be taking, but were not angry at this point.[21] They felt that the government deserved a reasonable chance. Also, they did not want to be too critical since Labour had so slim a majority in Parliament that it might face a new election at any time. They tried to avoid providing the Tories with any evidence that trade unionism was acting irresponsibly on economic affairs or had withdrawn support from its Labour party allies.

Therefore, despite the General Council's fears that the government was becoming more deflation-minded and that incomes policy might become a weapon against the TUC, the General Council agreed to carry on with the negotiations through the subsequent stages. Woodcock wanted the next stage to be concerned with the crucial question of the policy itself, but George Brown insisted he needed to establish the machinery to monitor price and incomes movements as quickly as possible as evidence that the government was making solid progress.[22] Woodcock relented, but the TUC was able to use the government's urgency as leverage to its advantage. As in 1947, the negotiations in early 1965 proceeded toward agreement because the Labour government maintained its unrelenting pressure on its trade union allies. At the same time, nevertheless, the TUC won a number of concessions on the details of that agreement.

The agreement for the creation of the National Board for Prices and Incomes (PIB) took only about two months to complete. As Brown had wanted, PIB was to examine cases of price and wage increases referred to it by the government. Neddy, however, where the TUC continued to hold strong influence, was to continue to hold the general responsibility for examining the broad questions of wage and price

20. *The Times* (London), January 28, 1965.
21. Mortimer interview, see *n.* 2.
22. Trades Union Congress, *Productivity, Prices, and Incomes,* p. 35.

movements. Most importantly, so far as the TUC was concerned, the conclusions reached by either the PIB or Neddy
would not be binding although the White Paper creating the
PIB indicated that the government would consider making
these findings binding if the voluntary system failed.[23]

The final stage in the three-part negotiations was the
most difficult, because it involved reaching agreement on a
specific policy for wage and price restraint. Negotiations
continued from the middle of February until the end of
March, and took place against a background of renewed concern that there might be yet another and more difficult run
on the pound during the spring if new trade figures showed
continued and perhaps even larger payments deficits. George
Brown repeatedly told the negotiators that the government
was eager to complete the last agreement as a matter of
urgency.[24] He wanted an agreement on a norm for price and
wage increases of between 3 and 3½ percent annually, primarily for its effect on the current rate of inflation and secondarily as part of the government's program to foster economic growth—thus reversing the negotiations' original priorities.

George Woodcock argued quite vehemently during this
last stage in the talks that this explicit shift in focus away
from the long-term purposes of the agreements was not only
a breach of faith but would inevitably pose a serious dilemma for both the TUC and the government.[25] He pointed
out that when Brown opted for the development of a longer-
term policy on incomes instead of imposing a short-term
freeze, he accepted the inevitable consequence that the rate
of wage increases would continue high for the present and
then then would wind down slowly, over a matter of months
or even years. By now urgently placing a 3 to 3½ percent
norm on wage increases in the face of months of increases
averaging between 8 and 10 percent, he was asking for a

23. Department of Economic Affairs, *Machinery of Prices and Incomes Policy,*
Cmnd. 2577 (February, 1965), p. 4.
24. George Woodcock, *loc. cit.*
25. Trades Union Congress, *Productivity, Prices, and Incomes,* p. 36.

dramatic and immediate turnabout that he obviously would not get. In addition, the TUC, by agreeing to the norm, stood to lose a great deal of credibility with its constituent unions and membership who were bound to consider the agreement as a sign that the General Council was selling out its interests to the government. The undercutting of TUC authority, moreover, would bode only more, not less, trouble for the government in gaining other agreements on the whole range of difficult economic policy issues.

George Brown did not directly refute Woodcock's objections. He noted that Woodcock was probably right that the achievement of a 3 to 3½ percent norm was unreasonable in the next few months, but he said that the government nevertheless had to present this norm as an example of its firmness.[26] The norm would be useful as a reference point in collective bargaining. Woodcock disagreed, but the General Council reluctantly agreed to accept the norm. In conclusion, Woodcock warned the negotiators that the government would use the unions' failure to meet this norm as an excuse for taking additional action.

As in the previous two stages of the negotiations, however, the TUC was able to use the leverage created by the government's impatience to extract important qualifying amendments to the norm. There could therefore be agreements for wage increases above the norm: (1) where higher productivity was achieved; (2) where the "national interest" dictated a change in the distribution of manpower; (3) where there was a "general recognition" that existing wage and salary levels were too low to "maintain a reasonable standard of living"; and (4) where differentials in wages had become proportionately unfair to groups of workers.[27] In addition, the agreement also provided for a government commitment to restrain the incomes of nonwage earners such as landlords and other self-employed people, and provided that Neddy

26. Sir Eric Roll, a director of the Bank of England and former Permanent Secretary of the Department of Economic Affairs. Interview, July 14, 1969.
27. Department of Economic Affairs, *Prices and Incomes Policy*, Cmnd. 2639 (April, 1965), p. 8.

would continue to examine the movements of such nonemployment incomes as profits.[28]

The General Council called a Conference of Trade Union Executives to meet in London on April 30, 1965, to ask for approval and support of the council's agreement on the three-part negotiations. In asking the conference to support the General Council's actions, George Woodcock concisely summed up the council's motivations for agreement:

> We cannot keep them [the Government] at arm's length. If we are not prepared to work wth Governments to make it possible . . . for them to fulfil their obligations, then they have two choices: either they will renege on their obligations and they will no longer accept the obligation to maintain full employment. Because of our inability or our unwillingness, whatever it may be, to fit our actions in with them, they will abandon or at best modify objectives which to us are desirable. Or, alternatively, they will not renege. They will say: "We are not going to be put on one side by the trade union Movement," and they will proceed to surround us with restrictions. They will move indirectly to circumscribe free bargaining and to restrain arbitration tribunals, and even consider extensions of the law to limit the right to strike and compel observance of contracts freely entered into. These are the directions in which a Government can move if they cannot move in the other direction with full co-operation.[29]

General Council leaders in 1948 had similarly argued that if the TUC did not agree to the wages freeze, the Attlee government would implement either more painful economic alternatives or would pass restrictive legislation. Woodcock's use of these same points in 1965 demonstrated the continuity of the response of at least the majority of the members of the General Council to the Labour government's demands for cooperation.

The Conference of Executives approved the council's actions by a "card vote" of more than 6 million to about 2 million. The vote represented a poll of only full-time trade union officials and not the rank and file, who, as George Woodcock suggested, would be as much the final judge of

28. Ibid., p. 9.
29. Trades Union Congress, *Productivity, Prices, and Incomes,* p. 39.

these agreements as they had been of Selwyn Lloyd's pay pause.

Trade Union Militancy. The approval of the elaborate agreements on prices, incomes, and productivity contrasted with the long years of stalemate on these issues during the Eden, Macmillan, and Home governments. The agreement again demonstrated the influence of the special relationship between the TUC and a Labour government. There still remained the question of whether the General Council could implement its commitment to restrain wages while raising productivity. Here, the General Council was treading on far more uncertain ground than the one-sided vote by the Conference of Executives to support the agreements indicated.

The authority of the General Council to direct positive action on incomes policy had never been tested during the long Conservative years because the council had repeatedly and firmly rejected any sort of agreement with the Tories. The only comparative precedent was the 1948–1951 period when the General Council effectively implemented a wages freeze that lasted for two and one-half years until it was eroded by the pressure of rising prices generated by Korean War-related shortages in 1951. The General Council's success during that period was due primarily to the dominance of exceptionally strong union leaders who controlled the largest unions in the TUC and believed firmly in close collaboration with the Labour party. Armed with the then extremely powerful argument that failure to support the government would bring on renewed depression as well as the loss of the social and economic gains that they believed only a Labour government could provide, Deakin, Lawther, Williamson, and the other leaders successfully marshaled support for the freeze.

In contrast, the leading figures in the trade union movement during the sixties were not nearly so able to dictate to their men, nor were they any longer so unanimous in their agreement with the government's views on economic policy.

The moderate faction, including Bill Carron, Sidney Greene, Lord Wright, and Sir Harry Douglass, still clearly dominated the General Council and usually carried a majority in favor of collaboration with the Wilson government—as was demonstrated repeatedly during the negotiations for the three-part agreement on prices, wages, and productivity. There was, however, a whole new generation of more "militant" trade union leaders finding their way to positions of leadership in a number of unions by their more critical approach to industrial relations and doubts about the value of what they called "uncritical" collaboration with the government-of-the-day.[30] Frank Cousins, although a bit older, had been the first such leader to join the General Council in 1956 when he succeeded Deakin, who had died the year before. Later Daniel McGarvey of the Boilermakers joined the council, and others like Hugh Scanlon of the Engineers and Jack Jones of the Transport Workers were gaining influential roles within their unions from which they were in position to take the leadership at the next chance.[31] (For example, Scanlon became the president of the Amalgamated Union in 1967 upon the retirement of the strong moderate leader, Bill Carron.)

The diminished influence of the moderate leadership on the council and the emergence of more militant leadership at every level of trade union administration was part of a broader struggle between militant and nonmilitant in the movement as a whole. The incumbency of a Labour government exacerbated this struggle because it more vigorously managed the economy and therefore pressed more insistently for union cooperation.

---

30. See especially the speech by Daniel McGarvey on prices and incomes policy. Trades Union Congress, *Report of Proceedings, Annual Trades Union Congress* (1966), pp. 467–468.
31. Jack Jones and Hugh Scanlon had been leaders at almost every level of their union organizations. Jones, who replaced Frank Cousins when he retired in 1969, had been a TGWU official since 1939, starting as a District Secretary and rising to be the union's Assistant Executive Secretary at the time of his election as General Secretary. Scanlon, on the other hand, had been a shop steward at the age of twenty-three and subsequently served as a Divisional Organizer and then became a member of the powerful Executive Committee in 1963 before he was elected to be the AEU President in late 1967.

The term "militant" is, however, difficult to define. V. L. Allen points out that the term "militancy" has a "strongly emotive connotation in the trade union movement."[32] Every trade unionist considers himself a militant in the sense that he believes he should press his power and influence and that of the movement as far as he feels that it can beneficially be pushed. In the context of the middle sixties, the term "militant" came to denote a union member or leader who was dissatisfied because he felt his union or the TUC had defined the boundaries to which they were willing to push too narrowly, and, in doing so, had sacrificed the interests of the movement. The militant trade unionist, for example, argued it was time for the trade union movement to press the unquestioned advantage in collective bargaining that full employment presented, rather than persisting in making agreements with government or private industry that compromised that advantage. Trade union leaders should only collaborate with government on economic policy, the militants argued further, when there was a direct and obvious advantage to be gained.

Militancy in the last decade was spawned by the rank and file and their shop stewards on the shop floor.[33] Far from the responsibilities of national leadership and the complicated questions of balance of payments and personal relationships with Labour party leaders, the shop stewards in particular have been less willing to listen favorably to arguments that they should exchange a wage freeze or restraint now, for a later *real* increase in the size and value of their men's pay. Their defeat of Lloyd's pay pause on the shop floor was not partisan, and their view of Labour's incomes policy was not partisan either.

The impatience of the rank and file with actions that restrained increases in their incomes or improvements in their working conditions was not a new phenomenon, though

32. Allen, *Militant Trade Unionism*, p. 18.
33. For an excellent study of the rise in the power of shop stewards and their influence on incomes policy, see Goodman and Whittingham, *Shop Stewards in British Industry*.

in the last ten years their opposition to wage restraint has stiffened considerably. The most significant change is that the views of the rank and file and their shop stewards have counted for much more. Their ability to influence the actual course of policy is much greater because an important by-product of full employment as well as the modernization and specialization of industry since the war has been the development of important workplace bargaining. More and more since 1945, national agreements in many industries, particularly in such "growth industries" as the automobile and chemical and engineering industries, have become only minimums from which plant level agreements departed to provide for much larger wage increases and other improvements.[34] Intense competition between employers competing for scarce labor and the ever present threat of unofficial (wildcat) strike action at a particular plant or throughout the industry placed shop stewards in a far more crucial position to determine the course of industrial relations in each plant and therefore to influence strongly the fate of commitments made by the national leadership in London. Full employment in this way limited the ability of the TUC to speak with authority on the most important economic issues, especially where commitments to action are involved.

Figure 7.1 documents the widening gap between actual weekly earnings and weekly wage rates. Goodman and Whittingham use this illustration to demonstrate the rapid development of significant plant level bargaining. Figure 7.1 also shows that "wage drift"[35] continued to intensify after Labour came to power in 1964 and demonstrates the failure of incomes policy under the terms of the three-stage agreement. The more insistently the Labour government focused on incomes policy as an immediate remedial measure, the

---

34. Turner, Clack, and Roberts, *Labour Relations in the Motor Industry*, chap. 5.
35. " 'Wage drift' means the difference between . . . earnings excluding overtime and the . . . wage rates arrived at as the result of wage negotiations and collective agreements. This drift is particularly noticeable in engineering, construction, shipbuilding and the electricity industries." Bailey, *Managing the British Economy*, p. 114.

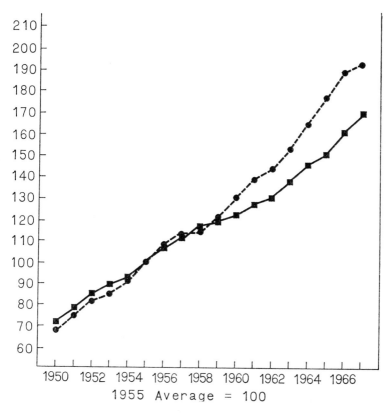

FIGURE 7.1 Weekly rates of wages and average weekly earnings for manual workers, 1950–1967. Source: Ministry of Labour, *Ministry of Labour Gazette*, 76 (May, 1968), 446.

more that incomes policy worked against the TUC's ability to deliver an effective incomes policy in any context.

The Sterling Crisis of 1965 and "Early Warning," July–September, 1965. The renewed sterling crisis which erupted on the heels of some very ominous trade figures in June, 1965 (see Table 7.1), prompted the government to reexamine urgently its anti-inflationary policies, including the operation of the voluntary incomes policy, although it had been scarcely two and one-half months since the final agreement had been reached. The breaches in that agreement were obvious (see Figure 7.1) and were due primarily to plant level agreements for wage rates above national settlements. The spectacle of the union's national leadership being defied on so large a scale presented the government with a difficult question about how to proceed to dampen inflation more decisively while retaining TUC cooperation on the whole broad range of economic issues. The government wanted also to find a way to enforce wage restraint without causing further erosion in the TUC's position with its rank and file membership.

At first, the Cabinet decided to avoid directly confronting the TUC with its failure to enforce the incomes agreement and chose instead to take, reluctantly, a more deflationary position.[36] On July 27 the Chancellor, James Callaghan, told Commons there would be new, tighter restrictions on borrowing for both consumers as well as industry. Also, he announced that the government would sharply limit local loan authority as well as reduce new government investments. When these measures failed to calm speculation in sterling and selling built to a new climax in August, the government rushed efforts to find new international credits, and to find a way to put some "bite" into their prices, incomes, and productivity agreements.

George Brown met with the General Council on August 26 to tell them that the government was considering a bill

---

36. For an account of the Wilson government's decision to turn to a more deflationary policy, see Brandon, chap. 9.

to authorize a compulsory "early warning" system under which the unions would be required to give the government advance notice of new wage claims, and business would similarly be required to give notice of prospective price increases.[37] The government, in turn, would be empowered to refer any claims or prospective price increases to the Prices and Incomes Board for examination. During the period that the PIB was investigating a claim (or increase), the claim would remain in suspension. In addition, Brown proposed to give the PIB statutory authority to require any information or evidence it felt was necessary to do its work.

The purpose of these measures, Brown said, was to put some "bite" into the voluntary incomes policy which clearly was not working.[38] He further asked that the General Council agree to act as if the bill had been enacted already pending its passage in the late fall after Parliament reconvened. He added confidentially that the government also needed this assurance because the Chancellor was currently negotiating with the American government for a new and substantial loan. The Americans, however, as well as Britain's European creditors, were demanding as a precondition to granting the new credits that the government move to toughen their anti-inflationary measures, especially against wage inflation.

George Woodcock again took the lead in answering Brown at this meeting. He was disturbed and angered by the proposal for early warning.[39] While still decidedly in favor of incomes policy in the context of economic growth and appreciative of the government's present difficult position, he felt the new proposals would only worsen the situation still further. He told Brown the government had already erred in placing too much emphasis on achieving an immediately successful incomes policy and especially by setting an unrealistic norm. This had placed the General Council in an untenable position with its membership, and early warning

37. Ibid., pp. 82–87.
38. Ibid., pp. 83–84.
39. Ibid., pp. 86–87.

would only make it more difficult to have any workable policy in the future. The men, he said, were in no mood to accept dictated agreements from above. In conclusion, he said he simply could not support early warning.[40]

Woodcock persisted in his refusal to cooperate and held the support of the majority of the council that day, despite the emotional pleadings of George Brown that the Americans were waiting for word of an agreement. By the time that Brown again met with the council on September 2 on the eve of the opening of the annual TUC Congress, however, the Cabinet had declared publicly its intention to legislate.[41] This removed the question of "whether to legislate" from the subsequent talks, but Brown still wanted the General Council to agree to act as though the legislation were already in force. Although the TUC leaders knew that the government would be certain to have the votes for passage, they were very aware that Brown also desperately needed agreement from the unions in order to present early warning as a credible policy.[42]

The meeting on September 2 lasted twelve hours. No one on the council, however moderate, had much taste for agreeing to this legislation which they feared would be only the first step toward the passage of debilitating restrictions on the whole framework of collective bargaining. Rather, moderate and militant factions (including Woodcock) argued over whether they could feasibly resist the government's plans.[43]

After hours of debate, the two factions on the council struck a compromise. The moderates led by Collison, Douglass, Carron, and O'Brien clearly held the majority in favor of coming to some sort of agreement with Brown.[44] Hill, McGarvey, and Woodcock, who had determinedly held out against agreement, finally consented to go along if the government would agree to introduce its legislation pending the

40. Ibid.
41. *The Times* (London), September 12, 1965, p. 12.
42. Sidney Greene, member of the General Council and General Secretary of the National Union of Railwaymen. Interview, July 24, 1969.
43. "Report from Brighton," *The Economist*, 216 (September 11, 1965), 962.
44. Brandon, p. 90.

success or failure of the TUC's own wage monitoring system that Woodcock suggested be established immediately.[45]

Congress debated "early warning" and the proposal to establish the TUC's own "wage vetting" system throughout the next day. In contrast to similar debates during the period of the Attlee government, and even in contrast to the debate at the Conference of Executives only six months earlier, the speakers for the General Council were sharply divided in their counsel to Congress.[46] George Woodcock, in his capacity as General Secretary, presented both sides of the argument, but clearly stated his dislike for the whole business. He urged the delegates to act pragmatically and, while supporting the agreement for legislation, to pass at the same time the resolution establishing the Incomes Policy Committee so that the TUC would have a "last chance" to demonstrate that trade unionism could responsibly take care of the question of wage increases itself. Woodcock told the delegates:

> We want to do this . . . so that we may be able to offset legislation which otherwise is threatened. . . . I am a believer in a prices and incomes policy, make no mistake about that. I believe, I have believed for a long time, in a prices and incomes policy. . . . I would like the T.U.C. to operate it because if we cannot, nobody can.
>
> If not, then the alternatives . . . become real possibilities . . . either you have a movement towards greater direction of the unions—and what do you think the Government's proposals are but greater direction of the unions? . . . or the state says the whole thing is unworkable and gives up the job of maintaining full employment and economic growth.[47]

TOWARD DEVALUATION

Congress finally approved the General Council's recommendation by a close vote of 5.3 million to 3.3 million. This

---

45. *The Times* (London), September 3, 1965, p. 10.
46. For example, see the speeches of Douglass, pp. 488–489; Cannon, pp. 486–487; McGarvey, pp. 473–475; and Woodcock, pp. 465–475; Trades Union Congress (1965).
47. Trades Union Congress (1965), p. 472.

vote demonstrated the deterioration in union support for the government, as well as for the General Council's leadership, when compared to the much wider margin by which the Conference of Executives approved the three-stage agreement only six months earlier.[48] Thus, a large minority of Congress registered its opposition to restraints on wage bargaining and also indicated an unwillingness to subject its wage bargaining intentions to TUC scrutiny.

This breach between the majority of the General Council and a large minority of Congress widened over the following two years. By continuing its collaboration on the wages issue, the General Council cut further ground from its position as a spokesman for trade unionism. The clearest indication of the council's weakness was the complete failure of the Incomes Policy Committee. From the beginning, the TUC's wage monitoring system was virtually paralyzed by a lack of information as well as a lack of resolve and ability to examine wage claims seriously. Although the committee examined more than 600 claims during its first nine months, it questioned only a handful and had no real effect on the course of any of them. The committee often acted on claims at the rate of fifty an hour during its one-day sessions each month.[49] It reached decisions to approve claims without making any attempt to measure them against the 3 to 3½ percent norm the TUC had agreed to honor. Most of the claims the committee approved were, in fact, far in excess of that norm.[50]

---

48. The Transport and General Workers' Union provided a large percentage of the opposition votes in both cases. In the latter vote, however, it picked up important support from the Electrical Trades Union, which has about 300,000 members, and support as well from many smaller unions. *The Times* (London), May 1, 1965, and September 9, 1965.
49. Douglass interview, see n. 5.
50. Lovell and Roberts, *A Short History of the T.U.C.*, p. 172. The General Council took the attitude that progress ". . . while not spectacular, had been much faster than they had anticipated . . ." and that the experience had confirmed ". . . that any attempt to impose too rigid a set of criteria on so heterogeneous a situation would inevitably break down under its own weight. . . . [T]he committee had been right to refrain from seeking to establish precise criteria, and in particular to reject any rigorous application of the White Paper's norm and criteria, and instead to adopt an empirical and explanatory approach." Trades Union Congress (1966), p. 314.

TABLE 7.1.   BALANCE OF PAYMENTS—Seasonally Adjusted, Current Account (£m)

Year	First Quarter	Second Quarter	Third Quarter	Fourth Quarter
1965	Even	−62	−29	+14
1966	−49	−63	−24	+179
1967	+32	−97	−2	−245

Source: Central Statistical Office. *Economic Trends.* London: H.M.S.O., 1970, p. xv.

The Prices and Incomes Board, during the same period from October, 1965, to July, 1966, worked far more diligently and efficiently, though still without significantly affecting the rate of wage increases that continued to average over 8 percent for the year. The board suffered not only from its newness and inexperience with the issues pertinent to the resolution of claims in each industry, but also by the limitations in the number of claims its relatively small staff could investigate. It tried in the few (twelve) cases it examined during those nine months to cover a wide range of occupations in order to provide a focus and standard that the TUC could then apply in the operation of its own voluntary system—but the TUC Committee was in no position to argue with its constituent national unions.

Wage inflation was therefore as intractable as ever when a forty-seven-day seamen's strike for sharply higher pay triggered the third and most severe balance of payments crisis of Labour's tenure during May, June, and July, 1966. (See Table 7.1.) The strike severely hurt Britain's precarious export business, but it was the 10 percent wage increase settlement that set off the disastrous run on the pound in July. This time the government wasted little time in trying to reach further agreements with the TUC. Instead, the Prime Minister told the General Council that his government planned to introduce, in addition to a package of deflationary measures, legislation to provide authority to impose a period of wage freeze to be followed by another period of severe wage restraint.[51] He added he very much wanted to

51. Trades Union Congress (1966), p. 307.

have the General Council's support, but he would proceed without that support.

Faced with the prospect of severe restrictive legislation, council members took even less time than they had in 1964 and 1965 to decide to "go along" with the Prime Minister's plans. In a long paper outlining its reasons for agreeing to the freeze, the council restated its disagreement with the government's deflationary measures which they said would end all hope that the *National Plan* could be fulfilled. They added, however, that despite their disagreement they had decided to support the government's plans in order to protect trade union interests.[52] Privately, council members believed, as in 1948, that they had no choice but to agree in order to retain any influence or access, and, more positively, that, if they did "go along," they might be able to use their continued alliance with Labour to at least mitigate the harshest portions of the government's freeze:

> It was only after the most scrupulous examination of the alternative courses of action genuinely open to them that the General Council reached the conclusion that the interests both of trade unionism and of the nation as a whole in the current critical situation, compelled them to acquiesce in the Government's proposal. In taking this decision the General Council understood and indeed shared the distaste with which trade unionists regard a standstill of up to twelve months in their incomes, but they did so in the belief that trade unionists will accept that at this time the needs of the nation must necessarily override sectional demands.[53]

The decision to approve the wage freeze strengthened the opposition to the General Council's leadership. The delegates to Congress in September, 1966, were even less impressed with the rationale for collaboration than they had been a year earlier. The vote to approve the General Council's Report on economic policy was a razor-thin 4.56 million to 4.22 million. Frank Cousins, only recently returned to his seat on the council after abruptly resigning from the government in protest against the wages freeze, led the opposition

52. Ibid., pp. 325–326.
53. Ibid., p. 323.

at Congress and scolded the TUC for its timidity and for its loss of perspective on what the council should do to protect the interests of the workingman:

> Conservative Governments have tried time and time again to put this [wage restraint] over to us. We have rejected it, although none of them have been as rigid as the one that has now been proposed. . . .
> Now we are being asked to accept this when the Government is a Government of our own choosing and one which we support. . . . To quote what has been said by Vic Feather [Assistant General Secretary of the TUC], we do not give them the right to have all the knowledge in the world, and we are an integral part of the Labour Movement and entitled to criticize our friends if they do not do the things we think they should be doing.[54]

The period of total and then severe restraint lasted for a full year, until August, 1967. When it expired, the government passed a new Prices and Incomes Act that gave them additional power to impose new delays of up to seven months on any prospective wage or price increase.[55] The General Council again went along. Despite George Woodcock's best efforts to explain the reasons for their agreement, Congress, in September, 1967, repudiated the agreement and then, with a majority of more than 1 million votes, condemned the government for its "intervention in collective bargaining as a solution to the country's economic problems.[56] Thus, Congress, in effect, told the General Council not to collaborate any further on incomes policy or to support government decisions that provided for further deflation.

CONCLUSION

Congress's admonishment against further collaboration did not become a serious impediment for the General Council, because the government finally devalued the pound two

---

54. Ibid., p. 464.
55. Department of Economic Affairs, *Prices and Incomes Policy After 30th June 1967*, Cmnd. 3235, March, 1967.
56. Trades Union Congress, *Report of Proceedings, Annual Trades Union Congress* (1967), pp. 521–522.

months later in response to a continuing run on sterling and bleak prospects for the economy in the foreseeable future. Devaluation made the issue of wages inflation less critical, although the government continued to stress the importance of restraint in helping Britain take full trading advantage of the new rate of exchange.

Nevertheless, Congress's action in repudiating its General Council was unique and highly significant. Its repudiation made explicit the growing pressure on the council to give priority to trade union interests.

The TUC's relationship with the Wilson government had been a sobering experience. The principal lesson for trade unionists was that it made little difference which party was in office. Despite Wilson's promise of a "new beginning," of economic expansion, and of rapidly rising living standards, Labour's conduct of economic policy was disappointingly like Tory "stop-go." The similarity included Labour's incomes policy which the government urgently pressed the TUC to accept, as the Tories had, in order to deal with repeated balance of payments crises.

The General Council's willingness, however reluctant, to honor its traditional loyalties to the Labour party as it did in 1948 in agreeing to the restraint of wages, provoked the conflict between the TUC and its membership. From the security of comparative material well-being and long years of full employment under governments of both parties, union members were far more concerned with gaining the benefits of full employment than with worrying about the loss of their jobs in a new depression. They measured the TUC's performance from a more pragmatic view, one that rejected incomes policy because it sacrificed the trade union movement's right to seek the best terms of employment. The shift of important collective bargaining to the shop floor allowed the membership in 1965 to translate its opposition to the agreements into effective rebellion.

The example of the failure of the 1964 and 1965 agreements on wage restraint indicated the membership would ignore TUC leadership in the future when it felt the council had unreasonably compromised those interests. Thus, the TUC's effective participation in economic decision making became more uncertain, and economic policy, in turn, became more vulnerable to paralysis. Traditional relationships between the TUC and the political parties continued to exercise some influence on the course of the TUC's participation in group politics. But the ineffectiveness of those 1964–1965 agreements testified to the impact that the convergence between the parties' programs had on reducing the chances that the TUC would be willing or able to cooperate with government on issues that required the compromise of vital trade union interests.

Collaboration or Conflict?

IN this study I have been principally concerned with examining the behavior of the Trades Union Congress in response to governmental efforts to manage the economy since the end of the Second World War. I have focused on Samuel Beer's argument that the position of such producer groups as the TUC has been greatly enhanced because government has increasingly needed their advice, acquiescence, and cooperation to realize the economic goals drafted by the wartime Coalition government as part of a new economic and social contract.[1] Beer comments that producer groups hold this power because they have the negative capability to disrupt public policy by refusing to perform their productive function.[2] The consequence has been that these groups now negotiate with government over the shape and implementation of public policy, a process that Beer calls the new group politics.[3] The successful conduct of producer group politics requires, however, that both government and the relevant producer groups be able and willing to reach and implement agreements. In order to accomplish these purposes, producer groups must be able to exercise effective leadership within their organizations in order to mobilize the consent of their memberships.

The development of the TUC as a more powerful producer group in its relations with government simultaneously both illustrates and modifies Beer's views about the new group politics. Government's management of the economy has drawn the TUC from the very fringes of power into the

---

1. Beer, *Modern British Politics,* p. 395.
2. Ibid., p. 320.
3. Ibid., p. 319.

center of economic decision making. The achievement of full employment especially, by the pressure it created for continuously higher wages, put the TUC into a crucial bargaining position. To mitigate the effects of Britain's chronic lack of resources and cyclical balance of payments problems, government tried to win TUC cooperation for the limitation of the growth of incomes to a rate of increase which was at least no greater than the rise in productivity.

The most salient points about the TUC's performance since 1945 have been that its power has been limited, and that it has had only negative influence on economic policy, especially on wages policy. Beer suggests that the power of producer groups to influence public policy varies with the extent of governmental attempts to manage the economy, and the intensity of the demands it makes for producer group cooperation.[4] Yet, contrary to Beer's argument, in the TUC's case government's demands for cooperation on wage restraint have steadily undermined the ability and willingness of the General Council to provide that cooperation. Thus, the TUC has become less rather than more influential. Specifically, the issue of wage restraint has generated enormous resistance within the trade union movement against the policy of TUC collaboration with government on incomes policy because wage restraint contradicts the fundamental purpose of the trade union movement to seek the best possible terms of employment.

The rationalization of policy, expressed in government's growing control over economic activity, thus forces the TUC to face repeatedly the question of whether to collaborate with government or to resist those demands and to continue its traditional struggle for immediate gains in wages and better working conditions. If the TUC were wholly insensitive to the milieu in which it functions, the answer would be simple: it would single-mindedly attend to the purposes of trade unionism and therefore relentlessly seek ever higher wages. The General Council, being at the center of eco-

---

4. Ibid., p. 209.

nomic decision making, and thus constantly exposed to the broader economic and social implications of trade union policy, however, faced continuous, strong pressure to shape trade union policies to serve the "national interest"—which governments of both parties have defined to include restraints on the growth of incomes.

This increasing pressure on the TUC to collaborate, first for temporary, and more recently for permanent incomes policy, has produced counter pressures from within the trade union movement on the TUC not only to resist government's demands but to press even more vigorously for higher wages. The resulting tensions between government and the TUC and between the TUC and its membership (both within the leadership and between the leadership and the rank and file) have gradually eroded the ability of the TUC to participate effectively in producer group politics. The TUC is not only more reluctant to make agreements for incomes policy but also less able to implement the agreements that it does make.

THE INFLUENCE OF PARTY RELATIONSHIPS

The examination in this study of the four cases—in 1947–48, 1956, 1961–1962, and 1964–1967—when governments sought to develop an incomes policy, demonstrates that the behavior of the TUC and its effect on the course of policy has been uneven. To a great extent, the behavior of the TUC has varied depending on the nature and force of the trade union movement's traditional relationship with the political party in office.

Governments of both parties—Conservative and Labour—have asked for greater collaboration since the war. But Labour governments, more committed to active intervention in the economy, have made greater and more insistent demands on the TUC. Nevertheless, in 1948 and in 1964–1965 the General Council reluctantly honored its alliance with Labour by promising the cooperation of the trade union movement, first, for a wages freeze, and, in the second example, for a comprehensive, permanent incomes policy. In contrast, the General Council consistently refused to reach any sort of agreement with Conservative governments on wage restraint. Largely because of trade unionism's traditional hostility for and distrust of the Tories, the General Council could reject Conservative pleas that the trade union movement serve the "national interest" by agreeing to incomes policies. While the Conservatives were in office the General Council instead gave primacy to trade union interests that dictated rejection of collaboration.

Both relationships, however, expose the limitations in TUC power. Labour governments have been able to force the General Council to agree to wage restraint without making substantial concessions to trade union interests. And, although Conservatives have been unable to win agreements from the TUC for incomes policy, the TUC's power has been solely negative. The TUC's veto which ended the negotiations in 1956, for example, did nothing to satisfy the positive demands of trade unionists for an expansionary economy and a higher standard of living. The collapse of those negotiations led to the immobilization of policy with subsequent damage to an already serious economic situation. To summarize, it has mattered little as far as the satisfaction of positive trade union interests are concerned which party has been in office, particularly as their economic policies have converged since the war. The TUC has been unable to convince governments of either party to adopt policies which they favor. Their power has been limited to vetoing Conservative policies it did not approve of, and primarily deflecting or delaying those of Labour. Thus, the TUC has been engaged in a series of defensive negotiations which it has hoped would prevent governments from successfully taking initiatives to restrain wages.

The TUC and Labour Governments. Relationships with Labour governments have been the more frustrating and disappointing for the TUC. The TUC strongly expects to be more influential under a Labour government than when the Tories are in office. Labour leaders themselves, when out of power, tend to encourage these feelings of comradeship and identity rooted in traditional class consciousness. Yet, in practice, the TUC enjoys no significant advantages in comparison to the more vigorous and insistent demands that Labour makes on the TUC for cooperation. The central point to be drawn about the relationship is that there is a fundamental incompatibility between the purposes of trade unionism and the plans and policies of Labour governments. Though never explicitly recognized by either side and submerged during periods when Labour is out of office, the conflict was evident in the two cases explored in this study.

The issue of incomes policy illustrates this point clearly because it has been central to the relationship between the TUC and Labour governments since the war. When Labour was out of office before 1945 and, again, before 1964, Labourite leaders collaborated with the TUC in formulating plans for economic reform—which gave the TUC influence on policy to the extent that Labour adopted those plans after it returned to office. In each case both sides recognized that the effective restraint of incomes would be crucial to the success of those plans. Yet, the restraint of incomes clashes fundamentally with the purpose of the trade union movement to seek increasingly higher wages. At the same time, the members of the General Council, particularly in 1964 and 1965, recognized that their membership would disapprove of wage restraint and that the TUC's directing authority was seriously limited by the autonomy of the constituent unions to take independent action. In both cases, however, the TUC participated in the formulation of those plans, only to face the problem subsequently, after Labour took office, of trying to deliver effective wage restraint.

In both 1948 and 1964, the General Council ultimately felt it had no choice but to succumb to the government's pressure for agreement because of the force of its traditional alliance with the Labour party. It agreed to a wages freeze in the first instance, and a comprehensive incomes policy in the second. But it was only in the first of the four cases examined in this study that the General Council implemented an effective incomes policy. The historical situation provided a uniquely strong rationale for collaboration in 1948. The council won the cooperation of its membership primarily because of the intensity of that crisis, which included a severe fuel shortage and then a sudden, brief surge of unemployment to over 2 million. This stirred still-fresh memories of the depression and fears of a return to Tory government—which was strongly identified in trade unionists' minds with bad times.[5] There seemed no alternative therefore but to support the Labour government. At that time trade unionists held high expectations for Labour policies. Only two years earlier the Labour government had swiftly initiated the economic reforms it had promised. These reforms included the nationalization of key sectors in the economy, which union members still expected would favorably transform the whole pattern of industrial relations. And now the Labour government promised that the 1948 wages freeze would be only a temporary measure to meet the emergency of that moment.

The General Council was not so fortunate in 1964–1965 when, after many years of exceedingly high employment and during a period of far greater material security, it was not able to press constituent unions to comply with its agreement for a more comprehensive and permanent, though milder, policy. The contradiction in the TUC-Labour alliance and the weakness of the TUC in its relationship with the government evoked a far stronger and more effective protest from the membership. George Woodcock's comments about the negotiations between the Wilson government and

---

5. Every older trade unionist interviewed, including Tewson, Geddes, Williamson and Douglass, indicated that the fuel crisis in 1947 and the subsequent surge of unemployment to over 2 million, even for only a few weeks, frightened them very badly. One of them said that he had not worked for three years during the depression and then only one week out of every four for about five years. He said that, having had that experience, which was not unusual, made him very willing to try to do whatever Attlee and his colleagues wanted to forestall another depression.

the TUC in 1964–1965 throws light on the limited influence TUC leaders felt they had, constricted by their continued loyalty to the Labour party.[6] Contrary to Beer's view, Woodcock contends that the bargaining process at that time, as well as later during Labour's incumbency, was more symbolic than real. Labour, it seemed to him, usually approached the General Council in order to win acquiescence for policies it had already rigidly committed itself to adopt. At these "discussions" Labour ministers preferred to limit themselves to the details of policy implementation rather than to argue matters of substance. The power that the TUC did have under those circumstances was the deflection and the delay of implementation of the harshest aspects of the policies that Labour was determined to enforce. Thus, although the TUC was able to win certain concessions from the Labour government they were not able to win from the Conservatives, the net force of Labour's policies was as painful and frustrating as were the consequences of the negotiations with the Tories.

The feeling of the union leadership at the lower levels and of the rank and file membership that the General Council was "caving in," "selling out," to the Labour government in 1964–1965 provoked local unions to ignore the TUC's agreements and pursue their own efforts for higher wages. The developments within the trade union movement in the sixties, in fact, demonstrated a growing awareness of the contradictions in the relationship between Labour and the trade union movement. Both a minority within the General Council and lower ranking trade union leaders, as well as the rank and file, were coming to recognize that the union movement was receiving little benefit from the political alliance with Labour, and that the convergence in economic policies between the two parties meant that whichever was in power demanded cooperation that clashed with the objectives of trade unionism.

6. George Woodcock, former Chairman of the Commission on Industrial Relations and former General Secretary of the TUC. Interview, July 17, 1969.

The TUC and Conservative Governments. The TUC has
been even less able to influence Conservative governments
than Labour ones. In neither the 1956 or the 1961 case was
the General Council able even to delay or deflect Conservative demands for wage restraint during the course of the
negotiations. In 1961, Selwyn Lloyd simply refused to discuss the question of his pay pause when the TUC raised the
matter during the negotiations over Neddy. However, for
the TUC, there were important, albeit negative, benefits in
this relationship because the lack of affective ties worked
both ways.

The principal advantage for the TUC in its relationship with the Tories was that, although a fundamental incompatibility existed between TUC and Conservative leaders and between Conservative demands for wage restraint and
the purposes of trade unionism, the absence of close ties
allowed the TUC to deal effectively with this incompatibility
by refusing to collaborate—a course of defiance it did not
feel it could follow with Labour in office. This veto power
not only forestalled the development of tension between the
TUC and its membership, but allowed the TUC to be a far
more negatively influential producer group with a Conservative government in office. Selwyn Lloyd recognized this
power when he tried to avoid a TUC veto of Conservative
wages policy by imposing the pay pause in the public sector
in the hope that private enterprise would follow suit.

Stalemate was sometimes part of TUC strategy in its
negotiations with the Tories, because its power was dependent on its exercise of negative influence. In the 1956 negotiations, for example, the TUC repeatedly spelled out its demand that prices be stabilized before the TUC would seriously consider agreeing to wage restraint. It repeated this
point several times and thereby gave tacit encouragement to
the Eden government's strategy of trying first to win a prices
agreement with the employers' organizations. Yet, although
the government was successful in winning the commitment
of a large number of businessmen for a prices freeze, the

TUC continued its opposition and vetoed the whole policy. In that instance, the TUC's demand for price restraint seemed to have been a ploy to create policy frustration which, in turn, provided a rationale for vetoing a government scheme that it didn't trust anyway.

Thus, the powerful influence that the TUC was able to exercise on the Conservative government worked in one direction and depended on the continuous rejection of change and a vigorous defense of the status quo. Ironically, when the TUC dealt with a Conservative government it more nearly assumed the position of strong leadership within the labor movement that is an essential requirement for successful producer group politics. Yet, its authority was predicated on its continued refusal to collaborate. To do otherwise would have immediately subjected the General Council to even more acrid charges of a sellout to "them" than were leveled against the TUC in 1964–1965 when it gave in to Labour.

The TUC's power in dealing with Conservative governments was thus strong but limited. At the same time, however, TUC leaders found the relationship much more satisfying than their relationship with Labour. Compared to the enormous pressure that a Labour government exerted to force them to agree to wage policies which clashed sharply with the purposes of trade unionism, their relative insensitivity to Tory anger made life a great deal easier, even though they continued publicly to profess their loyalty to Labour and their yearnings for its return to office:

Throughout the dark days of the Labour Government a surprising number of union worthies used to sigh secretly for those 13 wasted years of Tory misrule. . . .[7]

In summary, the TUC has not been influential in convincing either Labour or Conservative governments to adopt economic policies it favors. The TUC's power has been solely negative, being limited to a veto over Conservative

7. Torode, "Year of the Good Old Incomes Policy," *The New Statesman,* p. 4.

wages policies and the delay or deflection of Labour's. Its
relationship with Labour governments has been more frustrating and disappointing because, despite expectations of a
close working alliance, Labour has used these traditional
ties to force the General Council to agree to policies that
have been fundamentally incompatible with the purpose of
trade unionism. In contrast, the TUC's relationship with
Conservative governments has been easier because the General Council has been able to deal with the incompatibility
by rejecting collaboration.

INTERNAL UNION PRESSURES

In the sixties, the most important influence on the
TUC's behavior in its relationship with government was the
force of growing pressure from within the trade union movement on the TUC to refuse collaboration for wage restraint
and instead to push for a high wages policy. This pressure
has seriously weakened the ability of the General Council to
function effectively as a producer group spokesman. Beer
also recognizes this development in the Epilogue to the second edition of *Modern British Politics,* in his discussion of
the 1964–1966 crisis:

> The prolonged and intricate bargaining over this question
> by the Labour Government with producer groups, especially
> trade unions, makes a fascinating chapter in the history of func-
> tional representation. . . . At first glance this story illustrates
> the vast power of the great functional organizations of the mod-
> ern economy. Yet it would only be part of the truth to think of
> them as organizational giants grappling with representatives of
> the public interest. For these giants themselves are often not
> masters in their own houses.[8]

The erosion in the effectiveness of the TUC was mani-
fest in the shift in power away from the trade union center
back toward the shop floor. Full employment, as Beer points

8. Beer, p. 421.

out, compelled government to seek the advice and cooperation of the TUC for the restraint of wage inflation. Government's need of TUC consent dramatically enhanced the
power of the TUC in the relationship with government as it
was drawn into the center of economic decision making. Yet,
the terms of its participation in producer group politics
clashed with the TUC's purpose, which is to provide protection for its members' interests and the expansion of trade
union influence.

The convergence in the economic policies of both parties toward greater economic management, particularly the
development of economic planning, coupled with continued
full employment, progressively increased government demands on the TUC for cooperation for wage restraint. This,
in turn, sharpened the dilemma that the General Council
faced in deciding between conflict and collaboration. The
1964–1965 agreement was the most damaging to the council's
relationship with its members, both leaders and rank and
file. It added substance to the growing realization by the
leaders and membership that which party is in office makes
little difference, and that the TUC is both ineffective in
forestalling unwanted Labour policies and unable to influence governments of either party to pursue a high wages
policy. Some members of the General Council, but primarily lower level leadership and the rank and file, demanded that the General Council face squarely the contradiction of its concern with the "national interest," which
governments define to include a strong incomes policy, and
the purposes of trade unionism to seek continuously higher
wages. Their argument stressed the importance of winning
immediate, tangible gains in material welfare and rejected
the subtler and seemingly more abstract arguments about
the advantages of postponing wage increases now in order
to reap larger *real* gains at some unspecified later time. The
old slogan "power brings responsibility," they contended,
was an unsatisfactory rationale for justifying the TUC's
neglect of its proper role, which is to serve the direct interests of trade unionists rather than to negotiate their dilution.

The growing rejection of TUC leadership was based on the attitude expressed by one working trade unionist that "if the TUC or our own national leaders cannot or will not get us what we want, we will get it ourselves." This was far more than an idle threat. First, the defeat of the pay pause in 1961 and, more importantly, the successful defiance of the TUC's agreement for incomes policy in 1964–1965 provided telling evidence of the economic power held on the shop floor. Full employment had not only increased power at the center of the trade union movement, but it had also increased power, almost unnoticed until recent years, at the local levels as well. The very high level of employment with attendant shortages of highly skilled manpower created a bidding process in the factories in which employers agreed to pay wages, often under the duress of unofficial (wildcat) strikes, that were far above the national minimum. This power was largely unused until the last decade when dissatisfaction with national agreements began to increase. But its use in the late sixties has caused a shift in important economic influence away from the national level and exposed and played on the chronic internal weakness of the TUC.

The reorganization of the TUC in 1921 and later the explicit decision by the constituent member unions to retain their right to independent decision making after the failure of the General Strike seriously limited TUC authority. The TUC depended, therefore, as Bevin and Citrine clearly recognized, on winning power gradually from its member unions. It did so by virtue of the "services" it could perform, both defensively in protecting unions from government intentions or policy and, positively, by achieving greater influence for the union movement. The TUC acquired such status in collaborating with the Labour party to develop plans for economic reform in the thirties, an alliance which helped endow the trade union movement with a permanently stronger influence in economic decision making. The growth of TUC power over the years proceeded on this basis, stimulated by government intervention in the economy. However, the TUC's increase in power, both with the government and within the union movement, was not accomplished at the expense of the autonomy of its member unions nor was it immune to recall by them.

The more recent process in which power has been moving away from the trade union center first became important during the middle fifties when Frank Cousins was elected to the General Council and began to challenge the rationale for collaboration. This power shift took on vital significance during the 1964–1965 struggle. The process today involves the progressive diminution of TUC authority to deal with issues, like the wages issue, which are of vital importance to the constituent unions.

CONTRADICTIONS AND PROSPECTS

Beer concludes the second edition of his *Modern British Politics* by commenting that the further rationalization of policy and extension of planning is inevitable in "an economy that seeks both stability and expansion."[9] The further growth of functional representation is also inevitable, he argues, and will become "an even more important part of the representative system of the polity."[10] However, the analyses of the four cases presented in this study, considered with the experiences of the early seventies, indicate that the chances for the TUC's future successful participation in producer group politics are poor. There is, moreover, great doubt that the TUC ever really participated, in any of these cases, in what Beer would define as successful producer group politics. Beer's definition of the operational requirement for producer group politics is that both sides be willing to reach agreement and then that they be able to carry out their separate parts of the resulting bargain.[11] In the 1948 case only, however, did the TUC reach and effectuate an agreement, and then it did so under the duress of its loyalty to Labour and fears of renewed depression and a return to

---

9. Beer, p. 427.
10. Ibid.
11. Ibid., p. 421.

Tory government, but without resolving the substantive issues of the disagreement that were central to the negotiations. In all the other cases, the ultimate outcome was deadlock, and the government in each case had to implement an alternative means of dealing with the crisis.

The problem with the TUC's participation in producer group politics is that it is being asked to agree to a wage restraint which, if it were carried to its logical conclusion as a highly efficient and permanent policy, would essentially negate the original basic purposes for which the TUC and the trade union movement exist. Therefore, it is inevitable that at some point the TUC and its members down through the ranks will resist so fundamental a threat to their organization and interests. The developments during the sixties testified to the trade unionists' growing awareness of this problem and their impatience with incomes policies.

The prospects for the future also throw doubt on Beer's comments as they apply to the TUC. Anticollaboration pressures from within the union movement are likely to be applied against the TUC until tensions are resolved either by a change in TUC leadership or by a permanent alteration in the policy of full employment. With Conservative government led by Edward Heath in office in the early 1970s, the breach caused by the 1964–1965 example has been patched up to some extent by the struggle to deliver another veto against Tory wages policy. However, many national and local unions and their members continue to distrust the General Council and intend to continue making their own deals in the factories. The TUC is likely therefore to continue to lose authority to act as spokesman for the trade union movement on wages and other vital issues, and could eventually be left with only the "housekeeping" chores related to more routine responsibilities.

Over time, on the the other hand, there exists a strong possibility that the conflict within the trade union movement will be resolved by the emergence of a more militant majority on the General Council. This development will take a few years because most General Secretaries are elected to hold office until they reach retirement age or voluntarily step down. Already, the election of Hugh Scanlon of the Engineering Union and Jack Jones of the Transport Workers to succeed the retired Frank Cousins has given the council a more militant tone.

The dominance of militants on the General Council would reduce the possibility that the TUC would participate effectively in producer group politics. A militant majority would take a more pragmatic view of economic policy and exclude collaboration on the wages issue. A further result would probably be a significant weakening of the alliance between the TUC and a Labour government with the TUC moving towards a position of neutrality.[12]

These speculations about the future do nothing to offer optimism for more successful economic policy from the perspective of government. Clearly, the failure of incomes policy has contributed significantly to the poor showing of the British economy since 1945. Further, the growing unwillingness and inability of the TUC to cooperate on incomes policy is largely responsible. But it would be unreasonable to expect that the TUC could have implemented an incomes policy, except under conditions equaling the emergency of wartime.

The Heath government, taking office in 1970, implicitly recognized this dilemma during its first years by sharply departing from earlier Conservative wages policy. Bypassing the TUC, the government directly confronted the TUC's constituent unions at the contract bargaining table in the public sector. It tenaciously resisted each union's wage claims, provoking several long strikes during 1970 and 1971. The strategy was to lower gradually the rate of wage inflation by winning progressively smaller settlements. Further, the government sought to strengthen its hand and protect these agreements from wage drift by allowing unemployment to rise and proscribing unofficial strikes in the Industrial Rela-

12. This last point has also been made by Lovell and Roberts, *A Short History of the T.U.C.*, pp. 186–187.

tions Act, passed in late 1971 (which made wage contracts binding but only by mutual agreement).

By 1972, however, the Conservative strategy of confrontation was clearly in trouble. The disruptive postal and electricity strikes of the year before had been settled for increases that undermined the Conservative intention. Then, in early 1972, the long and disastrous coal strike halted nearly all industrial production. The miners only returned to the pits after the government agreed to pay an enormous wage increase of 20 percent.[13] Despite subsequent government warnings it would not agree to other such inflationary settlements, the confrontation strategy was in disarray much as the pay pause had been after Firemen were granted large increases in December, 1961.[14] Finally, with unemployment approaching one million, far beyond what government had expected, the Treasury hurried to reflate in order to reestablish full employment before the political consequences became disastrous.

Thus, as Britain prepared to join the European Economic Community in 1973, the Tory government continued to face the predicament of its relationship with the union movement and the TUC. The further rationalization of economic policy will inevitably further strengthen the influence of trade unionism. Government, as Beer comments, will therefore more urgently need the TUC's advice, acquiescence, and cooperation. Yet, the incompatibility between the terms of government's demands on the TUC for cooperation and the opposing pressure from within the union movement which undermine TUC authority remain unresolved. Until a solution can be found or until government fundamentally alters the goals of economic policy, the management of the economy and particularly the control of wages inflation will remain a very imperfect exercise.

---

13. Torode, "Miners Celebrate Victory," *Manchester Guardian Weekly*, February 26, 1972, p. 4.
14. Torode, "Everybody Now Special," *Manchester Guardian Weekly*, February 26, 1972, p. 4.

BIBLIOGRAPHY

PERSONAL INTERVIEWS, London, England

Allen, Alfred W. H., General Secretary of the Union of Shop, Distributive, and Allied Workers and a member of the General Council. July 22, 1969.

Blakenham, Lord (John Hare), retired former Minister of Labour. July 29, 1969.

Catherwood, Fred, Director-General of the National Economic Development Council. June 26, 1969.

Cobb, Martin, Confederation of British Industries. August 7, 1969.

Cousins, Frank, General Secretary, Transport and General Workers Union, and member of the General Council. Also former Minister of Technology from 1964 until 1966. August 5, 1969.

Donovan, Lord (Terence Norbert), retired Chairman of the Royal Commission on Trade Unions and Employers' Associations, 1965–1968. July 21, 1969.

Douglass, Lord (Harry Douglass), member of the Electricity Council. Former member of the General Council and Chairman of the TUC Economic Committee. July 15, 1969.

Feather, Victor, General Secretary of the TUC. August 26, 1969.

Geddes, Lord (Charles Geddes), retired former member of the General Council and General Secretary of the Post Office Workers. July 2, 1969.

Gray, Hugh, Member of Parliament. July 8, 1969.

Greene, Sidney, member of the General Council and General Secretary of the National Union of Railwaymen. July 24, 1969.

Jones, Aubrey, Chairman of the National Board for Prices and Incomes. July 11, 1969, and August 5, 1969.

Jones, Fred, Assistant Secretary with the Department of Economic Affairs and former member of the TUC's Economic Department. July 14, 1969.

Lea, David, member of the TUC's Economic Department. July 10, 1969.

Lloyd, Selwyn, member of Parliament and former Chancellor of the Exchequer. July 23, 1969.

Mortimer, James, member of the National Board for Prices and Incomes and former General Secretary of the Draughtmen's & Allied Technicians' Association. August 5, 1969.

Murray, Len, Assistant General Secretary of the TUC and former head of the TUC's Economic Department, 1948–1969. July 31, 1969.

Nield, Sir William, Permanent Secretary to the Department of Economic Affairs. July 7, 1969.

Roll, Sir Eric, a director of the Bank of England and former Permanent Secretary of the Department of Economic Affairs. July 14, 1969.

Shanks, Michael, former Co-ordinator of Industrial Policy in the Department of Economic Affairs and Economic Correspondent for the *Sunday Times*. July 25, 1969.

Smith, Ron, member and Managing Director (Personnel and Social Policy) of the British Steel Corporation, former General Secretary of the Union of Post Office Workers, and member of the TUC General Council. June 27, 1969.

Tewson, Vincent, retired former General Secretary of the TUC, 1946–1960. August 11, 1969.

Tomlinson, George, member of the Research Department of the Amalgamated Union of Engineering & Foundry Workers. July 23, 1969.

Walsh, Michael, member of the TUC's International Department. August 21, 1969.

Williamson, Lord (Tom Williamson), retired former member of the General Council and General Secretary of the National Union of General and Municipal Workers. July 2, 1969.

Woodcock, George, former Chairman of the Commission on Industrial Relations and former General Secretary and Assistant General Secretary of the TUC, 1960–1969. July 17, 1969, and August 21, 1969.

UNPUBLISHED TUC DOCUMENTS

TUC Economic Committee. "Report (First Section) by TUC Staff on Economic Expansion and Planning," No. EC 7/2 (April 12, 1961). (Mimeographed.)

———. "Report (Second Section) by TUC Staff on Economic Expansion and Planning," No. EC 8/3 (May 26, 1961). (Mimeographed.)

———. "Supplement Report (First Section) by TUC Staff on Economic Expansion and Planning," No. EC 8/6 (May 26, 1961). (Mimeographed.)

———. "Supplement Report (Second Section) by TUC Staff on Economic Expansion and Planning," No. EC 8/8 (May 26, 1961). (Mimeographed.)

TUC General Council. "The Government's Economic Measures," No. EC 11/5 (August 9, 1961). (Mimeographed.)

———. "Meeting between Economic Committee and Chancellor," No. GC 15/2 (August 23, 1961). (Mimeographed.)

TUC Economic Committee. "Minutes of the First (Special) Meeting Held at Congress House on 27th September, 1961," No. EC (Special) 1 (September 27, 1961). (Mimeographed.)

TUC Economic Committee. "The National Economic Development
   Council," No. EC 2/6 (October 11, 1961). (Mimeographed.)
———. "Economic Planning—Report of Meeting between the Chancellor and the Economic Committee 25th October, 1961," No. EC
   3/3 (November 8, 1961). (Mimeographed.)
———. "Recent Economic Developments," No. EC (Special) 2/1 (No-
   vember 28, 1961). (Mimeographed.)
———. "The Government's Wages Policy," No. EC (Special) 2/2 (No-
   vember 28, 1961). (Mimeographed.)
———. "Economic Situation—Letter from Chancellor of the Ex-
   chequer," No. EC (Special) 2/3 (November 28, 1961). (Mimeo-
   graphed.)
———. "Meeting between the Chancellor and Economic Committee,"
   No. EC 4/5 (December 13, 1961). (Mimeographed.)
———. "Economic Situation—Letter from Chancellor of the Exchequer
   24th November, 1961," No. EC 4/9 (December 13, 1961). (Mimeo-
   graphed.)
———. "Wage Restraint and a National Incomes Policy—Chancellor's
   Statement," No. EC 5/2 (January 10, 1962). (Mimeographed.)
———. "Meeting between the Chancellor and Economic Committee,"
   No. EC 5/5 (January 10, 1962). (Mimeographed.)
———. "The Purpose in Joining the N.E.D.C.," No. EC 6/7 (Febru-
   ary 14, 1962). (Mimeographed.)

PUBLISHED TUC DOCUMENTS

Trades Union Congress. *Report of Proceedings, Annual Trades Union
   Congress,* 1924; 1925; 1927–1934; 1937; 1938; 1940; 1942–1945;
   1947–1969. London: Trades Union Congress.
———. *Trade Unionism and the Control of Industry.* London: Trades
   Union Congress, 1932.
———. *Post-War Reconstruction.* London: Trades Union Congress,
   1944.
———. *Interim Report on the Economic Situation.* London: Trades
   Union Congress, 1947.
———. *Trades Union Structure and Closer Unity.* London: Trades
   Union Congress, 1947.
———. *Report of the Special Conference of Trades Union Executives
   on May 25, 1940.* London: Trades Union Congress, 1940.
———. *Report of Proceedings at a Special Conference of Executive
   Committees of Affiliated Organizations, March 24, 1948.* London:
   Trades Union Congress, 1948.
———. *ABC of the TUC.* London: Trades Union Congress, 1954.
———. *Productivity, Prices and Incomes* (1965). London: Trades Union
   Congress, 1965.
———. *Productivity, Prices, and Incomes: Report of a Conference of
   Executive Committees Held on 30th April 1965.* London: Trades
   Union Congress, 1965.

———. *Conference of Affiliated Organizations of the Trades Union Congress, Incomes Policy. . . .* London: Trades Union Congress, 1967.

———. *Incomes Policy (1967).* London: Trades Union Congress, 1967.

———. *Trade Unionism.* London: Trades Union Congress, 1967.

———. *Action on Donovan.* London: Trades Union Congress, 1968.

———. *Economic Review 1968.* London: Trades Union Congress, 1968.

———. *Economic Review and Report of a Conference of Executive Committees of Affiliated Organisations 1968.* London: Trades Union Congress, 1968.

———. *Equal Pay.* London: Trades Union Congress, 1968.

———. *Productivity Bargaining.* London: Trades Union Congress, 1968.

———. *The History of the T.U.C. 1868–1968.* London: Trades Union Congress, 1968.

———. *Economic Review 1969: Report of Conference.* London: Trades Union Congress, 1969.

BOOKS

Alexander, Ken, and John Hughes. *Trade Unions in Opposition.* London: Fabian Society, 1961.

Allen, V. L. *Power in Trade Unions.* London: Longmans, 1954.

———. *Trades Unions and the Government.* London: Longmans, 1960.

———. *Trade Union Leadership.* London: Longmans, 1957.

———. *Militant Trade Unionism.* London: Merlin Press, 1966.

Bailey, Richard. *Managing the Economy.* London: Hutchinson, 1968.

Ball, R. J., and Peter Doyle (eds.). *Inflation.* Harmondsworth, England: Penguin Books, 1969.

Barov, Noel. *Recent Trends in British Trade Unions.* New York: League for Industrial Democracy, 1945.

Bassett, Reginald. *The Essentials of Parliamentary Democracy.* London: Macmillan, 1935.

Beer, Samuel. *Treasury Control.* Oxford: Clarendon Press, 1956.

———. *British Politics in a Collectivist Age.* New York: Knopf, 1965.

———. *Modern British Politics.* Second edition. London: Faber & Faber, 1969.

Beveridge, Sir William. *Social Insurance and Allied Services.* New York: Macmillan, 1942.

———. *Full Employment in a Free Society.* London: Allen & Unwin, 1944.

Bevin, Ernest, and G. D. H. Cole. *The Crisis.* London: The New Statesman and Nation, 1931.

Birkenhead, Lord (Frederick Winston Furneaux Smith). *Walter Monckton.* London: Weidenfeld and Nicolson, 1969.

164 BIBLIOGRAPHY

Blackburn, Robert M. *Union Character and Social Class.* London: Batsford, 1967.
Blackburn, Robin, and Alexander Cockburn (eds.). *The Incompatibles: Trade Union Militancy and the Consensus.* Harmondsworth, England: Penguin Books, 1967.
Boyd, Francis. *Richard Austin Butler.* London: Rockliff, 1956.
Brady, Robert A. *Crisis in Britain.* Berkeley, Calif.: University of California Press, 1950.
Brandon, Henry. *In the Red.* Boston: Houghton Mifflin, 1967.
Brittan, Samuel. *Steering the Economy.* London: Secker & Warburg, 1969.
Brunner, John. *The National Plan: A Preliminary Assessment.* London: Institute of Economic Affairs, 1965.
Bullock, Alan. *The Life and Times of Ernest Bevin.* 2 vols. London: Heinemann, 1960, 1967.
Butler, David E. *The British General Election of 1955.* London: Macmillan, 1955.
———. *The British General Election of 1951.* London: Macmillan, 1952.
———. *The Electoral System in Britain Since 1918.* London: Oxford University Press, 1963.
———, and Jennie Freeman. *British Political Facts 1900–1967.* London: Macmillan, 1968.
———, and Donald Stokes. *Political Change in Britain: Forces Shaping Electoral Change.* New York: St. Martin's Press, 1969.
Butler, R. A. *Fundamental Issues.* London: Conservative Political Centre, 1946.
Cairncross, Alexander Kirkland. *Factors in Economic Development.* London: Allen & Unwin, 1962.
———. *Some Problems of Economic Planning.* Beograd [England]: Foreign Trade Research Institute, 1957.
Castles, Francis G. *Pressure Groups and Political Culture.* London: Routledge & Kegan Paul, 1967.
Caves, Richard E., and Associates. *Britain's Economic Prospects.* Washington, D.C.: The Brookings Institution, 1968.
Christoph, James B. *Britain at the Crossroads.* New York: Foreign Policy Association, 1967.
Churchill, Winston. *A Four Years' Plan for Britain/ The Prime Minister's Broadcast Speech.* London: The Times Publishing Company, 1943.
———. *Their Finest Hour.* Boston: Houghton Mifflin, 1949.
———. *Mr. Churchill's Declaration of Policy to the Electors.* London: S. H. Benson, 1945.
Citrine, Lord (Walter Citrine). *Men and Work.* London: Hutchinson, 1964.
———. *Two Careers.* London: Hutchinson, 1967.
Clegg, H. A. *Labour in Nationalized Industries.* London: Fabian Society, 1950.
———. *Industrial Democracy and Nationalization.* Oxford: Blackwell, 1951.
———, A. J. Killick, and Rex Adams. *Trade Union Officers.* Cambridge: Harvard University Press, 1961.

———. *British Economic Policy Since the War.* Harmondsworth, England: Penguin Books, 1958.

Shrimsley, Anthony. *The First Hundred Days of Harold Wilson.* London: Weidenfeld and Nicolson, 1965.

Sidebotham, Herbert. *Labour's Great Lie.* London: Hutchinson, 1945.

Skidelsky, Robert. *Politicians and the Slump.* London: Macmillan, 1967.

Snowden, Philip. *Wages and Prices.* London: The Faith Press, 1920.

Steele, David B. *More Power to the Regions.* London: Fabian Society, 1964.

Stewart, J. D. *British Pressure Groups.* Oxford: University Press, 1958.

Stewart, Michael. *An Incomes Policy for Labour.* London: Fabian Society, 1963.

———. *Keynes and After.* Harmondsworth, England: Penguin Books, 1967.

Stout, Hiram M. *British Government.* New York: Oxford University Press, 1953.

Turner, Ben. *About Myself.* London: H. Toulmin, at the Cayme Press, 1930.

Turner, H. A., Garfield Clack, and Geoffrey Roberts. *Labour Relations in the Motor Industry.* London: Allen & Unwin, 1967.

Titmuss, Richard M. *Essays on 'The Welfare State.'* London: Allen & Unwin, 1966.

———. *Income Distribution and Social Change.* London: Allen & Unwin, 1962.

Wigham, Eric. *What's Wrong with the Unions?* Baltimore: Penguin Books, 1961.

———. *Trade Unions.* London: Oxford University Press, 1956.

Wilson, Harold. *The New Britain.* Harmondsworth, England: Penguin Books, 1964.

Woolton, Frederick James Marquis. *Memoirs.* Second edition. London: Cassell, 1959.

Warswick, G. D. N., and P. H. Ady (eds.). *The British Economy 1945–1950.* Oxford: Clarendon Press, 1952.

———. *The British Economy in the Nineteen-Fifties.* Oxford: Clarendon Press, 1962.

ESSAYS IN COLLECTIONS

Beer, Samuel. "The British Legislature and the Problems of Mobilizing Consent," *Lawmakers in a Changing World*, Elke Frank, ed. Englewood Cliffs, N. J.: Prentice-Hall, 1966. Pp. 30–48.

Christoph, James B. "The Birth of Neddy," *Cases in Comparative Politics*, James B. Christoph, ed. Boston: Little, Brown, 1965. Pp. 44–89.

Wertheimer, Egon. "Portrait of the Labour Party," *Studies in British Politics*, Richard Rose, ed. New York: St. Martin's Press, 1966. Pp. 34–48.

PERIODICALS

Beer, Samuel. "Pressure Groups and Parties in Britain," *American Political Science Review*, 50 (March, 1956), 1–23.
————. "British Planning under the Labor Government," *Social Research*, 17 (March, 1950), 35–64.
————. "The Comparative Method and the Study of British Politics," *Comparative Politics*, 1 (October, 1968), 19–36.
Citrine, Walter. "The Month," *Labour*, 6 (June, 1944), 290.
Clegg, Hugh. "Making An Incomes Policy Work," *Socialist Commentary*, February, 1965, pp. 5–7.
————. "What's Wrong with Incomes Policy?" *Socialist Commentary*, February, 1966, pp. 5–7.
Daly, Lawrence. "Protest and Disturbance in the Trade Union Movement," *The Political Quarterly*, 40 (October-December, 1969), 447–453.
The Economist, 141 (July 12, 1941), 38–39, "Wages and the War Effort."
————, 154 (February 21, 1948), 291–292, "Exorcising the Symptoms."
————, 154 (April 24, 1948), 662–667, "Notes of the Week."
————, 170 (February 13, 1954), 439–441, "Mr. Butskell's Dilemma."
————, 176 (August 20, 1955), 595–596, "Wages or Prosperity."
————, 213 (November 28, 1964), 943–945, "The Sterling Test"; 1041–1044, "Seven Days That Shook Sterling."
————, 216 (September 11, 1965), 296–963, "Report from Brighton."
Flanders, Allan. "Wages under a Labour Government," *Socialist Commentary*, January, 1958, pp. 5–7.
Fox, Allan. "Criticizing the Trade Unions," *Socialist Commentary*, January, 1960, pp. 16–19.
Godwin, B. Anne. "The TUC in Changing Times," *Socialist Commentary*, March, 1963, pp. 18–20.
Headly, Bruce. "Trade Unions and National Wages Policy," *The Journal of Politics*, 32 (May, 1970), 407–439.
Hemming, M. F. W., C. M. Miles, and G. F. Roy. "A Statistical Summary of the Extent of Import Control in the United Kingdom Since the War," *The Review of Economic Studies*, 26 (February, 1959), 75–109.
Hughes, John. "The Facts about Unemployment," *The New Statesman*, October 22, 1971, pp. 530–532.
Labour, November, 1951, p. 65.
————, September, 1956, pp. 167–168, "The President's Point of View."
Marsh, Arthur. "Give Shop Stewards Their Due," *Socialist Commentary*, February, 1960, pp. 17–19.
The New Statesman, November 26, 1971, pp. 717–718, editorial, "970, 022: A New Style Emerges."
Pennock, J. Roland. "Agricultural Subsidies in England and the United States," *American Political Science Review*, 56 (September, 1962), 621–633.
Shanks, Michael. "Planning: How to Do It in Britain," *Socialist Commentary*, November, 1961, pp. 9–11.

Socialist Commentary, October, 1950, pp. 218–220, "Commentary on Trade Union Congress."
———, May, 1950, pp. 108–111, editorial, "Limits of Wage Restraint."
———, September, 1958, pp. 2–4, editorial, "Planning without a Plan."
———, September, 1961, pp. 3–5, editorial, "All Planners Now?"
———, February, 1962, pp. 3–5, editorial, "Planning through the Looking-Glass."
Torode, John. "Year of the Good Old Incomes Policy," *The New Statesman*, January 1, 1971, pp. 4–5.
———. "Unions Face Up to the Bill," *The New Statesman*, April 2, 1971, p. 450.
———. "The Road from Blackpool Pier," *The New Statesman*, September 10, 1971, p. 319.
———. "Everybody Now 'Special,'" *The Manchester Guardian Weekly*, February 26, 1972, p. 4.
———. "Miners Celebrate Victory," *The Manchester Guardian Weekly*, February 26, 1972, p. 4.
Walker, P. C. Gordon. "TUC and Post-War Reconstruction," *Labour and Trade Bulletin*, 79 (October 5, 1944), 5–6.
Webber, W. J. P. "Trade Unions and the Tories," *Socialist Commentary*, 18 (March, 1954), 60–63.
Williamson, Sir Thomas. "Are the Unions Irresponsible?" *Socialist Commentary*, December, 1957, pp. 4–5.

GOVERNMENT PUBLICATIONS

Great Britain

Central Office of Information. *Britain's Economic Position.* Special Briefs Section. London: H.M.S.O., 1947.
Central Statistical Office. *Economic Trends.* London: H.M.S.O., 1970.
———. *Monthly Digest of Statistics.* June, 1950. London: H.M.S.O., 1950.
———. *Monthly Digest of Statistics.* July, 1954. London: H.M.S.O., 1954.
———. *Monthly Digest of Statistics.* December, 1954. London: H.M.S.O., 1954.
———. *Monthly Digest of Statistics.* July–December, 1956. London: H.M.S.O., 1956.
———. *Monthly Digest of Statistics.* July–December, 1957. London: H.M.S.O., 1957.
———. *Monthly Digest of Statistics.* January–June, 1958. London: H.M.S.O., 1958.
———. *Monthly Digest of Statistics.* July–December, 1960. London: H.M.S.O., 1960.
———. *Monthly Digest of Statistics.* July, 1961. London: H.M.S.O., 1961.
———. *Monthly Digest of Statistics.* November, 1961. London: H.M.S.O., 1961.

Central Statistical Office. *Monthly Digest of Statistics.* December, 1961. London: H.M.S.O., 1961.

———. *Monthly Digest of Statistics.* July-December, 1962. London: H.M.S.O., 1962.

———. *Monthly Digest of Statistics.* July-December, 1964. London: H.M.S.O., 1964.

———. *Monthly Digest of Statistics.* July-December, 1965. London: H.M.S.O., 1965.

———. *Monthly Digest of Statistics.* July-December, 1966. London: H.M.S.O., 1966.

———. *Monthly Digest of Statistics.* December, 1967. London: H.M.S.O., 1967.

Department of Economic Affairs. *Prices and Incomes Policy.* Cmnd. 2639 (April, 1965). London: H.M.S.O., 1965.

———. *Machinery of Prices and Incomes Policy.* Cmnd. 2577 (February, 1965). London: H.M.S.O., 1965.

———. *Prices and Incomes Policy after 30th June 1967.* Cmnd. 3235 (March, 1967). London: H.M.S.O., 1967.

———. *The National Plan.* London: H.M.S.O., 1965.

———. *Prices and Incomes Policy: An "Early Warning" System.* Cmnd. 2808 (November, 1965). London: H.M.S.O., 1965.

———. *Prices and Incomes Standstill: Period of Severe Restraint.* Cmnd. 3150 (November, 1966). London: H.M.S.O., 1966.

———. *Prices and Incomes Standstill.* Cmnd. 3073 (July, 1966). London: H.M.S.O., 1966.

———. *Productivity, Prices and Incomes Policy in 1968 and 1969.* Cmnd. 3590 (April, 1968). London: H.M.S.O., 1968.

Department of Employment and Productivity. *In Place of Strife: A Policy for Industrial Relations.* Cmnd. 3888 (January, 1969). London: H.M.S.O., 1969.

The Economic Situation: A Statement by Her Majesty's Government. October 26, 1964. London: H.M.S.O., 1964.

House of Commons. *Parliamentary Debates,* vol. 351 (September 5, 14, 15, 1939), cols. 507–530, 755–798, 907–916.

———. *Parliamentary Debates,* vol. 432 (February 7, 1947), cols. 2183–2184.

———. *Parliamentary Debates,* vol. 433 (February 10–28, 1947).

———. *Parliamentary Debates,* vol. 434 (March 10, 1947), cols. 970–971 and 193.

———. *Parliamentary Debates,* vol. 441 (August 6, 1947), cols. 1499–1517.

———. *Parliamentary Debates,* vol. 447 (February 12, 1948), cols. 592–602.

———. *Parliamentary Debates,* vol. 545 (October 26, 1955), cols. 202–236.

———. *Parliamentary Debates,* vol. 548 (February 17, 1956), cols. 2675–2681.

———. *Parliamentary Debates,* vol. 551 (April 17, 1956), cols. 850–893.

———. *Parliamentary Debates,* vol. 644 (July 10–24, 1961).

———. *Parliamentary Debates,* vols. 645–646 (July 25, 1961), cols. 218–229.

——. *Parliamentary Debates,* vol. 649 (November 21, 1961), cols. 1145–1147.

——. *Parliamentary Debates,* vol. 651 (December 18, 1961), cols. 981, 986–987.

——. *Parliamentary Debates,* vol. 701 (November 4, 1964), cols. 214–234.

——. *Parliamentary Debates,* vol. 701 (November 11, 1964), cols. 1025–1046.

——. *Parliamentary Debates,* vol. 717 (July 27, 1965), cols. 228–232.

Ministry of Reconstruction. *Employment Policy.* Cmd. 6527 (May, 1944). London: H.M.S.O., 1944.

National Board for Prices and Incomes. *General Report April 1965 to July 1966.* Report No. 19. Cmnd. 3087 (August, 1966). London: H.M.S.O., 1966.

——. *Productivity and Pay During the Period of Severe Restraint.* Report No. 23. Cmnd. 3167 (December, 1966). London: H.M.S.O., 1966.

——. *Productivity Agreements.* Report No. 36. Cmnd. 3311 (June, 1967). London: H.M.S.O., 1967.

——. *Second General Report July 1966 to August 1967.* Report No. 40. Cmnd. 3394 (August, 1967). London: H.M.S.O., 1967.

——. *Third General Report August 1967 to July 1968.* Report No. 77. Cmnd. 3715 (July, 1968). London: H.M.S.O., 1968.

——. *Fourth General Report July 1968 to July 1969.* Report No. 122. Cmnd. 4130 (July, 1969). London: H.M.S.O., 1969.

National Economic Development Council. *Productivity Prices & Incomes: A General Review 1966.* London: H.M.S.O., 1967.

——. *Productivity Prices & Incomes: A General Review 1967.* London: H.M.S.O., 1968.

——. *Productivity Prices & Incomes: A General Review 1968.* London: H.M.S.O., 1969.

——. *Conditions Favorable to Faster Growth.* London: H.M.S.O., 1963.

——. *The Growth of the Economy.* London: H.M.S.O., March, 1964.

——. *Growth of the United Kingdom Economy to 1966.* London: H.M.S.O., 1963.

National Incomes Commission. *Report on the Scottish Plumbers' and Scottish Builders' Agreements of 1962.* Cmnd. 1994 (April, 1963). London: H.M.S.O., 1963.

——. *Remuneration of Academic Staff in Universities and Colleges of Advanced Technology.* Report No. 3. Cmnd. 2317 (March, 1964). London: H.M.S.O., 1964.

——. *Agreements of November-December 1963 in the Engineering and Shipbuilding Industries.* Report No. 4 (Final). Cmnd. 2583 (February, 1965). London: H.M.S.O., 1965.

Prices and Incomes Act 1967. 15 Eliz. 2, chapter 53.

Prices and Incomes Act 1968. 16 Eliz. 2, chapter 42.

Prime Minister. *The Economic Implications of Full Employment.* Cmd. 9725 (March, 1956). London: H.M.S.O., 1956.

Prime Minister. *Statement on Personal Incomes, Costs, and Prices.*
Cmd. 7321 (February, 1948). London: H.M.S.O., 1948.
Royal Commission on Trade Unions and Employers' Associations.
Minutes of Evidence. 18 (Tuesday 25th January 1966). Witness:
Department of Economic Affairs. London: H.M.S.O., 1966.
———. *Minutes of Evidence.* 61 (Tuesday 29th November 1966) and
65 (Tuesday 31st January 1967). Witness: Trades Union Congress. London: H.M.S.O., 1967.
———. *Report: 1965–1968.* Cmnd. 3623 (June, 1968). London:
H.M.S.O., 1968.
*Statement on the Economic Conditions Affecting Relations between
Employers and Workers.* Cmd. 7018 (January, 1947). London:
H.M.S.O., 1947.
Treasury. *National Income and Expenditure of the United Kingdom.*
London: H.M.S.O., 1956, 1957, 1959, and 1960.
———. *Economic Report on 1967.* London: H.M.S.O., 1968.
———. *Economic Survey for 1947.* Cmd. 7046 (February, 1947). London: H.M.S.O., 1947.
———. *Economic Survey 1956.* Cmd. 9728 (March, 1956). London:
H.M.S.O., 1956.
———. *Economic Survey 1958.* Cmnd. 394. London: H.M.S.O., 1958.
———. *Economic Survey 1961.* Cmnd. 1334. London: H.M.S.O., 1961.
———. *Economic Survey 1962.* Cmnd. 1678. London: H.M.S.O., 1962.
———. *Incomes Policy: The Next Step.* Cmnd. 1626 (February, 1962).
London: H.M.S.O., 1962.

United States of America

United States Department of Commerce. *British Wages.* Washington
D.C.: Government Printing Office, 1926.

PARTY PUBLICATIONS

Boyle, Sir Edward. *Conservatives and Economic Planning.* London:
Conservative Political Centre, 1966.
Conservative Party. *Conservative Party Conference* (1947). London:
Conservative and Unionist Central Office, 1947.
———. *Conservative Party Conference* (1950). London: Conservative
and Unionist Central Office, 1950.
———. *Conservative Party Conference* (1951). London: Conservative
and Unionist Central Office, 1951.
———. *Conservative Party Conference* (1956). London: Conservative
and Unionist Central Office, 1956.
———. *Party Policy at a Glance.* London: R. Anscombe, 1950.
———. *The Industrial Charter.* London: Conservative and Unionist
Central Office, 1947.
———. *The Right Road for Britain.* London: Conservative and
Unionist Central Office, 1949.
Conservative Political Centre. *Economic Recovery: Productivity,
Wages, and the Trade Unions.* London: Conservative Political
Centre, 1967.

Conservative Research Department. *Background to the Budget*, No. 7. London: Conservative Central Office, April 7, 1969.
———. *Dead-end Budget 1969*. No. 8. London: Conservative Central Office, May 12, 1969.
———. *Prices and Incomes Theory*. London: Conservative Central Office, September 23, 1968.
Labour Party. *Constitution* (Adopted 1918). London: Labour Party, 1919.
———. *Full Employment and Financial Policy*. London: Labour Party, 1944.
———. *Let Us Face the Future*. London: Labour Party, 1945.
———. *Challenge to Britain*. London: Labour Party, 1953.
———. *Repeal of the Trade Disputes Act*. London: Labour Party, 1946.
———. *Plan for Progress*. London: Labour Party, 1958.
Labour Research Department. *Wages, Prices and Profits*. London: Labour Publishing Company, 1922.

NEWSPAPERS

Numerous articles were examined in the following newspapers:

The British Worker (London)
Daily Herald (London)
The Financial Times (London)
The Guardian (Manchester)
The New York Times
The Times (London)
The Washington Post

PAMPHLETS

Bray, Jeremy. *The New Economy*. Fabian Tract 362. London: Fabian Society, July, 1965.
Brittan, Samuel. *Inquest on Planning in Britain*. Vol. 33. London: Political and Economic Planning, January, 1967.
A Fabian Group. *Socialism in the Sixties: A Plan For Incomes*. Fabian Research Series 247. London: Fabian Society, April, 1965.
Hughes, John. *An Economic Strategy for Labour*. Fabian Tract 372. London: Fabian Society, March, 1967.
McCarthy, William. *Socialism in the Sixties: The Future of the Union*. Fabian Tract 339. London: Fabian Society, September, 1962.
Pigou, A. C. *The Transition from War to Peace*. Oxford Pamphlets on Home Affairs. London: Oxford University Press, 1943.
Shanks, Michael. *Is Britain Viable?* Fabian Tract 378. London: Fabian Society, December, 1967.

Stewart, Michael, and Rex Winsbury. *Socialism in the Sixties: An Incomes Policy for Labour.* Fabian Tract 350. London: Fabian Society, October, 1963.

Turner, H. A. *Is Britain Really Strike-Prone?* University of Cambridge Department of Applied Economics, Occasional Papers: 20. Cambridge: Cambridge University Press, 1969.

Wilson, Harold. *Post-War Economic Policies in Britain.* Fabian Tract 309. London: Fabian Society, September, 1957.

Woodcock, George. *The Trade Union Movement and the Government.* Leicester: Leicester University Press, 1968.

UNPUBLISHED MATERIALS

Lloyd, Selwyn. "N.E.D.C. and Parliament" (August 12, 1963). (Mimeographed.)

Sirkin, Gerald. "The 1949 Devaluation of the Pound Sterling." Unpublished Ph.D. dissertation, Columbia University, New York, 1956.

Warner, Aaron N. "British Trade Unionism under a Labor Government, 1945–1951." Unpublished Ph.D. dissertation, Columbia University, New York, 1954.

INDEX

Atlee, Clement, 31, 39, 66, 78
  government, 6, 53, 56, 59–60, 62, 85
  wages bargain of 1948, 70

Baldwin, Stanley
  government, 17
Beaver, Hugh, 102–3
Beer, Samuel, 53, 70, 159
  new group politics, 144
  pluralistic stagnation, 7
  producer group politics, 4–5, 51, 71,
    144, 145, 153–54, 156–57
  wages bargain of 1948, 52
Beveridge Report *(Report on Social
  Insurance)*, 44–45
Beveridge, Sir William, 44, 47
Bevin, Ernest
  and Beveridge Report, 45
  and Coordination Committee, 13
  foreign secretary, 66
  and General Strike, 19
  and Second World War, 35, 39–43
  and TUC, 20, 21, 33, 34, 49, 155
Birch, Alan, 84
Boyle, Sir Edward, 103
British Employers' Confederation, 87,
  92
Brown, Ernest (Minister of Labour),
  35–36
Brown, George (Deputy Prime Minister and Secretary of State for
  Economic Affairs), 118
  critical of trade unionism, 120–21
  and Department of Economic Af-
    fairs, 118
  and early warning, 134–36
  negotiations with TUC, 122, 124–27
Butler, R. A., 75, 76, 81, 82
"Butskellism," 76

Cairncross, Alec, 103
Campbell, Jim, 84
Carron, Bill, 130, 136

Chamberlain, Neville
  government
    and rearmament, 34–35
    and TUC, 36–39
Churchill, Winston
  government, 39, 81–83
    appoints Bevin, 39
    and Beveridge Report, 45
    and TUC, 81, 82–83
Citrine, Lord (Walter Citrine)
  Chamberlain government, 36, 38
  and General Strike, 17, 19
  and TUC, 20, 21, 33, 34, 40, 49, 155
Clynes, J. R., 11
Coal Commission Report (1926), 17
Conference of Trade Union Executives
  approves negotiations with Labour
    (1965), 128, 137, 138
  and General Strike, 18, 19
  and National Joint Advisory Com-
    mittee, 37
  wages bargain of 1948, 67
Conservative (government), 6, 7
  contrasted with Labour in wages
    bargaining policy, 73–74, 85–86,
    89, 91, 94–96
  economic planning with TUC,
    101–2, 104–7, 113, 114, 115
  economic policies, 74–78, 87, 98,
    101–6
  era of good feelings with TUC, 81–
    84
  negotiations with TUC in 1956,
    85–86, 88–91, 93–96
  and the pay pause, 97, 104, 106,
    107–13, 114, 151
  and price stability, 85–86, 87, 92–93,
    94
  review of relationships with TUC,
    151–53
  similarity to Labour's economic
    policies, 76, 78, 117
  and TUC in 1970's, 157–59
Control of Employment Bill, 36–37

INDEX

Strikes *(continued)*
  and Conservatives, 83, 158–59
  General Strike, 16–21
  and the pay pause, 110, 111
  seamen's, 139
  strengthen TUC, 10–13
Swales, Alonzo, 15

Taxes
  and Conservatives, 79, 87, 98, 104
  and Labour, 123
  TUC's reactions to, 88–89
Tewson, Vincent, 60
  cooperation with government, 61,
    121, 149n
  wage restraint, 63, 66
Thomas, J. H., 17, 19
The Times (London), 108, 111
Trade Disputes Act, 23
*Trade Unionism and the Control of
  Industry* (TUC), 28–30
Trades Union Congress (TUC)
  conflict with General Council, 141–
    43
  Coordination Committee, 13
  gains strength, 10–13, 34, 38, 43,
    49
  and the General Strike, 16–21
  internal union conflicts, 153–56
  Parliamentary Committee, 13
  and post Second World War, 47–50,
    52, 84
  and rearmament, 34–38
  reorganized, 13–14, 15–16
  and the Second World War, 43, 47–
    49
  structure of, ix–x, 30
  and trade union interests, 7, 20–21,
    63, 74, 115, 134, 145–46, 150,
    153–56, 157

and trade union militancy, 116–17,
  131–32, 142–43
Transport and General Workers
  Union, 13, 84
Treasury Agreement (1915), 10–11
Turner, Ben, 21. *See also* Mond-
  Turner talks

Unemployment, 14, 58, 63, 99, 159

Wages drift, 132, 158
Wages policies
  Conservatives, 82, 83, 85–86, 94, 97,
    109–10, 112, 113, 151, 158–59
  General Council, 63, 64, 121, 124,
    128, 136–37, 148–49
  Labour, 59, 60, 61–62, 63, 65, 118,
    124, 126–27, 134–35, 148
  TUC, 5–7, 52, 56, 74, 126–28, 138,
    145–46, 157
Wages bargain of 1948, 52, 60–61, 62–
  72, 73
Williamson, Lord (Tom Williamson),
  149n
  cooperation with government, 61,
    71n, 129
  wage restraint, 65
Wilson, Harold, 100
  government, 116, 117–18
Woodcock, George
  and early warning, 135–37
  negotiates with Conservatives, 105,
    106, 110, 111–12
  negotiates with Labour, 122, 124–
    28, 149–50
  position in trade union movement,
    121
  profile, 120